CityPack
Brussels
& Bruges

**ANTHONY SATTIN &
SYLVIE FRANQUET**

*Anthony Sattin is the author of
several books and is a regular
contributor to the* Daily
Telegraph *and* The Sunday
Times. *Sylvie Franquet is a
linguist, has worked as a
model, translator and tour
manager, and writes a column
for the Belgian newspaper* De
Morgen. *Together they wrote
the AA Explorer Guides to*
Egypt *and the* Greek Islands.

Brussels area map, top
Central Brussels map,
bottom
Bruges centre map
on inside backcover
←

AA Publishing

Contents

About this book

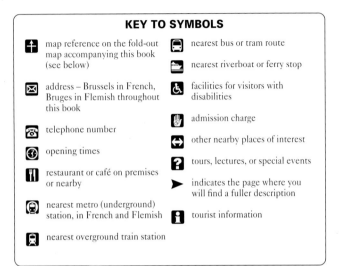

KEY TO SYMBOLS

➕ map reference on the fold-out map accompanying this book (see below)

✉ address – Brussels in French, Bruges in Flemish throughout this book

☎ telephone number

🕓 opening times

🍴 restaurant or café on premises or nearby

🚇 nearest metro (underground) station, in French and Flemish

🚉 nearest overground train station

🚌 nearest bus or tram route

⛴ nearest riverboat or ferry stop

♿ facilities for visitors with disabilities

✋ admission charge

↔ other nearby places of interest

❓ tours, lectures, or special events

➤ indicates the page where you will find a fuller description

ℹ tourist information

CityPack Brussels & Bruges is divided into six sections to cover the six most important aspects of Brussels and Bruges.

- An overview of the cities and their people
- Itineraries, walks and excursions
- The top 25 sights to visit
- Features about different aspects of the cities that make them special
- Detailed listings of restaurants, hotels, shops and nightlife
- Practical information

In addition, easy-to-read side panels provide fascinating extra facts and snippets, highlights of places to visit and invaluable practical advice.

CROSS-REFERENCES
To help you make the most of your visit, cross-references, indicated by ➤, show you where to find additional information about a place or subject.

MAPS
The fold-out map in the wallet at the back of the book has a comprehensive street plan of Brussels with an inset of Bruges city centre. All the map references given in the book refer to this map. For example, the Hôtel de Ville in the Grand' Place in Brussels has the following information: ➕ E7 indicating the grid square of the map in which the Hôtel de Ville will be found.

The city-centre maps found on the inside front (Brussels) and back (Bruges) covers of the book itself are for quick reference. They show the top 25 sights in the two cities, described on pages 24–48, which are clearly plotted by number (**1**–**25**, not page number) from west to east in each city.

BROUWERY

BRUSSELS
& BRUGES
life

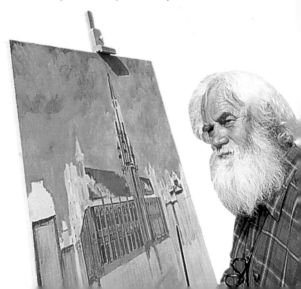

INTRODUCING BRUSSELS & BRUGES

The Grand' Place in Brussels carpeted with flowers, a display created every other year

Brussels and Bruges share a historical heritage. Both grew and prospered as medieval trading towns, as their magnificent surviving squares and palaces will testify. But it is their contrasting features, representing the twin-identity of Belgium, that draws visitors to them. Modern Brussels is the larger, busier and more commercially-orientated city, while Bruges has remained largely untouched since the 16th century when the silting of the Zwin river blocked her trading routes. Culturally they are divided by their roots – Flemish-speaking Bruges is in Flanders, while Brussels borders predominantly French Walloonia – and rivalry endures between those who speak Flemish and those who speak French. The cities are quintessential tastes of Belgium and if you visit Brussels, don't miss the opportunity of a trip to Bruges, 100km to the northeast and only an hour's train ride away.

A great king

Although Belgium is a democracy led by a prime minister, King Baudouin I, who died in 1993, did much to unify the country. He made a stand on matters where his principles were at stake: during the 1990 abortion debate he found himself unable to sign the law, so abdicated for a day to allow it to be passed.

There is officially no such thing as a capital of Europe, but Europeans talk about Brussels in much the same way as Americans refer to Washington. This is not only because the European Parliament is there (Strasbourg and Luxembourg share that distinction) but because it is home to the European Commission, the 'Eurocrats', who often appear to be the driving force behind the European ideal. Brussels can look forward to a future as one of the world's centres of political power, yet the urge to flow with the European tide has not been cost free. The city is changing too fast and in the wrong direction for some residents. High salaries, low taxes, long vacations, big cars, easy hours and well-padded expense accounts are reckoned to be a Eurocrat's lot.

Bruges, a city of canals

The Eurocrats have spawned a cosmopolitan Euro-neighbourhood of cafés, restaurants and pubs. There are even shops selling all manner of souvenirs stamped with the European symbol: a circle of 12 gold stars on a blue background. Nearby Square Ambiorix and Square Marie-Louise enclose an ornamental park complete with fountain, pool and grottos, where the civil servants take their ease. Beyond this modern image of the city, however, Brussels is a vibrant place with an exciting buzz, a keen interest in culture, superb restaurants and specialist shops. At heart it is a city of traders who have always placed a high value on the arts. As a result, with its architecture, its visual arts and its performances of music, theatre and dance, Brussels has enough to keep you busy for this visit, and your next one, too.

If Brussels is Belgium's political capital, then Bruges is the tourist capital. The reason for Bruges' popularity is obvious when you stroll

City of bridges

No name could fit the city better than 'Brugge,' Flemish for 'bridge.' The city had its origins around a bridge over the canal (*reie*), probably the Blind Donkey bridge. To protect the crossing, a borough was built and the city gradually grew around it. Bruges still has about 80 bridges, several of them masterpieces of medieval architecture.

*Brussels lace – one of
the city's specialist shops*

Regional
variations

It's not just language that divides
Belgians into their region – there
are regional parliaments as well as
the national parliament. Great
efforts are made by the central
government to avoid showing
favouritism, often with absurd
results: when money was allocated
for roads in the northern region of
Flanders, for instance, the southern
region of Wallonia received identi-
cal funding, even though this
resulted in one highway ending in
the middle of a field.

around the centre. As one of Europe's best-
preserved medieval cities, it is blessed with a
wealth of medieval art and architecture, good
food and a head-spinning variety of
excellent beer.

Bruges is easy to enjoy. Distances are
small and the city is ringed with parks
and cut through by canals. Set these
against a backdrop of medieval buildings and cobbled streets, add horse-
drawn carriages, church bells and
working windmills, and you have the
perfect place to step back in time for a
few days.

Bruges is a city of seasons. Go for a
walk on a Sunday in winter when the
shops and cafés are closed and the
empty streets heavy with melancholy,
and you will understand why the writer George
Rodenbach called the city *Bruges la morte* (dead
Bruges). In mid-summer Bruges is transformed
and you are unlikely to find a moment's soli-
tude. It is then that *Bruggelingen* talk of their city
as a victim of its own popularity.

When it comes to fine food Belgium has long
lived in the shadow of France. However,
Belgian cuisine is among the finest in Europe,
and both Brussels and Bruges boast some excellent restaurants. Whether it is a simple croissant
and hot chocolate for a light breakfast to start
the day, a waffle and coffee mid-morning, *moules*
(mussels) at midday, or *frites* bought from a stand
in the middle of the night, food is taken seriously by the Belgians. The traditional dishes in
both cities, such as *waterzooi* (fish or chicken
stew), *stoemp* (vegetable or meat purée) and
fresh sole and *crevettes* (shrimps), were all originally country fare. Modern Belgian cuisine is
based on peasant traditions, although what is
served in both Brussels and Bruges is more
cosmopolitan, more sophisticated and refined.
Whatever the rivalry in Brussels and Bruges,
you will eat well.

THE CITIES IN FIGURES

BRUSSELS

Population
- 1991: 954,045 Belgians in Brussels
- 80 per cent of Bruxellois are French-speakers, 20 per cent Flemish
- One in four people living in Brussels is a foreigner

Tourism
- 1995: Visitors (tourists and businessmen) spent 5,040,390 nights in Brussels

Food and drink
- Brussels has around 1,800 restaurants
- 1,000 beers offered at Chez Moeder Lambic Bar (not all in stock at the same time)

Environment
- 13.8 per cent of Brussels is green, making it the world's second greenest capital (after Washington)

First
- 1835: First train railway track on mainland Europe (inaugurated by King Leopold I)

BRUGES

Population
- Around 120,000 people live in Bruges and surrounding parishes

Tourism
- Bruges is Belgium's No. 1 tourist destination
- It attracts some 2.5 million visitors each year
- 1995: Visitors (tourists and businessmen) spent about a million nights in Bruges

Heritage
- More than 150 monuments in the city have been protected

CHRONOLOGIES

BRUSSELS

AD 695	Brocsella (Brussels) is first mentioned on the trade route between Cologne and Flanders.
979	Charles, Duke of Lorraine, moves to St-Géry (central Brussels), founding the city.
1459	Philip the Good, having inherited Flanders and Burgundy, brings Brabant and Holland under his control and settles in Brussels.
1515	Charles V, soon to become Holy Roman Emperor and King of Spain and the Netherlands, arrives in Brussels and stays until he abdicates in 1555.
1568	The beheading of the Independence fighters Counts of Egmont and Horne sparks a revolt that leads to the independence of the United Province of the Netherlands from Spain, but not of present-day Belgium, which becomes known as the Spanish Netherlands.
1695	French forces attack Brussels, destroying some 4,000 buildings.
1713–94	Under Austrian Hapsburg rule, Brussels is captial of the Austrian Netherlands.
1795	Brussels under French rule.
1815	After Napoleon Bonaparte's defeat at the Battle of Waterloo, Brussels reverts to the Dutch.
1830	The Belgian Revolution leads to independence and the crowning of Leopold of Saxe-Coburg as King of the Belgians.
1957	Brussels becomes headquarters of the EEC.
1967	Brussels is made headquarters of NATO.
1992	Belgium becomes a federal state.
2000	Brussels: European City of Culture.

BRUGES

3rd century AD	Bryggja is established, named for a key bridge.
1127	The first walls go up around Bruges.
1302	A French army is defeated by Flemish craftsmen and peasants at the Battle of the Golden Spurs. By this time, Bruges has become one of the world's great trading cities.
1303	The first-known procession of the Holy Blood.
1384	Philip the Bold, Duke of Burgundy, inherits Flanders and ushers in a period of prosperity and great cultural and political changes.
1468	Charles the Bold, Duke of Burgundy and son of Philip the Good, marries Margaret of York in Damme.
1488	An uprising against Archduke Maximilian the Hapsburg heir who tried to limit the city's privileges leads to his kidnap and three months detention in Bruges. The reprisals against the Bruges burghers begin the steady decline of the city when Maximillan became emperor in 1493.
1516	Genoese and Florentine traders, who had set up business ventures in Bruges under a treaty of 1395, move to Antwerp.
1550	Bruges loses access to the sea with the silting up of what is now known as the Zwin.
1898	Flemish is officially recognised as the country's joint-language with French.
1907	New Boudewijn Canal links Bruges again with the port of Zeebrugge, which creates industrial development.
1950s	Flourishing industrial sector near the sea, but the city's mainstay is tourism.
2002	Bruges: European City of Culture.

PEOPLE & EVENTS FROM HISTORY

Jan van Eyck

Famous modern Belgians

King Albert (crowned in 1993)

King Baudouin I (reigned 1951–93)

Jacques Brel, who sang passionately about his country

Hugo Claus, Nobel literature prize nominee, author of *The Sorrow of Belgium*

Jean-Claude van Damme, action-movie star

Johnny Halliday, rock star

Hergé's Tintin, whose adventures are translated into 51 languages

Eddy Merckx, bicycle hero

Toots Thielemans, Mr Jazz.

JAN VAN EYCK

One of the masters of Renaissance painting and generally credited as the father of Flemish painters, van Eyck (*c*1390–1441) mastered the technique of perspective well ahead of his Italian contemporaries. As well as being a painter, van Eyck was also a diplomat and chancellor to King Philip the Good. Like film director Alfred Hitchcock, he is famed for including little self-portraits in his pictures. In one of his most famous works, the *Arnolfini Wedding Portrait*, the artist can be seen in the mirror. It was in Bruges that van Eyck painted his *Adoration of the Lamb* (1432), later to adorn the cathedral in Ghent.

RENÉ MAGRITTE

René Magritte (1898–1967) was one of the original members of the Surrealist Movement that was founded in Paris in the mid-1920s. Returning from France to his native Belgium in 1927, he created a body of work that was always very precise and technically perfect. Apart from the three years spent in Paris his entire career was spent in Brussels. Magritte remained true to surrealism throughout his career juxtaposing the ordinary with the startling and the disturbing as demonstrated in his works in the Musée d'Art Moderne (▶ 33).

LEOPOLD II

The second King of the Belgians, Leopold II (1865–1909) reshaped Brussels, laying broad new avenues from the historic centre to the royal domain and palace. The Cinquantenaire complex and its Arc de Triomphe, which celebrated 50 years of Belgian independence, show his ambition. But he will also be remembered as the ruler of the Belgian Congo, a territory almost half the size of Europe, which was 'offered' by the explorer Henry Morton Stanley. Leopold ruled the Congo as his personal domain, in a reign that was marked by mass murder and atrocities. In 1908, a year before his death, Leopold was forced to hand over administration of Congo to the Belgian parliament.

BRUSSELS
& BRUGES
how to organize your time

ITINERARIES

Both Brussels and Bruges can easily be explored on foot. Note that most museums and sights in Belgium close over lunch time and that many museums close on Mondays in Brussels and on Tuesdays in Bruges. Opening times of smaller museums can be erratic; check before visiting.

ITINERARY ONE	**BRUSSELS: ROUND THE GRAND' PLACE**
Morning	Start by exploring the different guildhouses on the Grand' Place (► 28) and check the times for the morning guided tour of the Hôtel de Ville (► 29). If there is a wait, join the crowds staring at Manneken Pis (► 27) or visit the Musée de la Ville Bruxelles (► 50).
Lunch	Have a light lunch in the art-nouveau café Le Falstaff (► 68) or in one of the restaurants overlooking the Grand' Place.
Afternoon	Walk through the rue des Bouchers and the elegant Galeries St-Hubert up to the cathedral of St Michael and Ste Gudule (► 36). On the way back, visit the Centre Belge de la Bande Dessinée in the art nouveau Magazins Waucquez (► 37). In the early evening, take a stroll past Brussels' famous cafés (► 68).
ITINERARY TWO	**BRUSSELS: FROM ART TO SHOPPING**
Morning	Start with the neighbouring musées d'Art Ancien et Moderne (► 32–33) and stroll through the place Royale (► 34) to the place du Grand Sablon, with its impressive Church of Notre Dame du Sablon and the pretty gardens of the Petit Sablon (► 30).

Wittamer patisserie in the Grand Sablon

Lunch	Possiblities include Le Pain Quotidien (➤ 64), L'Ecailler du Palais Royal (➤ 62), and Au Stekerlapatte (➤ 64).
Afternoon	Take a tram to the Musée de Victor Horta (➤ 31). Discover some of the city's finest art-nouveau architecture in the St-Gilles area and then window-shop on the avenue Louise (➤ 35).

ITINERARY THREE — BRUGES: THE HISTORIC CENTRE

Morning	Climb the belfry on the Markt (➤ 46) for a good overview of Bruges. Continue to the Burg (➤ 47) and visit the Brugse Vrije museum and the astonishing Gothic room in the Town Hall, and then on to the Heilig Bloedbasiliek (➤ 48).
Lunch	Walk to the Huidenvettersplein where there are several fish restaurants with a terrace.
Afternoon	Follow the Dijver to the Groeninge Museum (➤ 45) and after that the Gruuthuse Museum (➤ 44). Wander around the garden towards the Onze-Lieve-Vrouwekerk (➤ 43). In the evening, walk along the romantic floodlit canals or take a boat trip (➤ 19).

ITINERARY FOUR — BRUGES: PEACE, QUIET AND CANALS

Morning	Start the day at Kathedraal St-Salvator (➤ 40) and follow with the Memling Museum (➤ 42) and some of the best Flemish art. Walk to the peaceful Begijnhof (➤ 41) and enjoy the quiet.
Lunch	Have lunch in the Wijngaardplein or take a picnic to the park overlooking the Minnewater (➤ 57) – there are good shops to buy picnic food in nearby Katelijnestraat.
Afternoon	Walk along the canals (➤ 59). The Dijver, Groenerei, and Verversdijk lead to the Potterierei, and then visit the lesser-known Museum Onze-Lieve-Vrouw Ter Potterie (➤ 51). Return along the Kruisvest and visit the Sint-Janshuysmolen windmill (➤ 55).

WALKS

THE SIGHTS

- Grand' Place (➤ 28)
- Plaques to Charles Buls (Mayor and restorer of the Grand' Place) and Everard't Servaes (14th century defender of Brussels' liberties)
- Manneken Pis (➤ 27)
- Église Notre-Dame du Bon-Secours
- Janneken Pis (panel ➤ 27)

INFORMATION

Distance 1.5km
Time 1–2 hours
Start point Grand' Place
⊞ E7
🚇 Gare Centrale/Centraal Station or Bourse/Beurs
🚋 Tram 23, 52, 55, 56, 81
End point Rue des Bouchers
⊞ E7

Fish restaurants abound near place Ste-Catherine

THE CRADLE OF BRUSSELS, FROM MANNEKEN TO JANNEKEN PIS

Leave the Grand' Place via rue Charles Buls, passing two plaques under the arcade. Walk along rue de l'Etuve leading to Manneken Pis, then turn right into rue des Grands-Carmes to the Marché du Charbon. Walk past Église Notre-Dame du Bon-Secours to the boulevard Anspach. There turn right, walk to the traffic lights and cross left into rue des Riches Claires with a 17th-century church. Turn right into the street leading to place St-Géry where, immediately left, a passageway leads to the back of the church and the original site of the River Senne.

Return to the square where a plaque on a renovated 19th-century covered market indicates the site of Brussels' origins. Walk along rue du Pont de la Carpe and then left into rue Antoine Dansaert where there are restaurants and clothes shops. Take a right into rue du Vieux Marché aux Grains, leading to place Ste-Catherine, built on the basin of Brussels' old port, which explains why there is still a fish market and many fish restaurants. Walk past the Tour Noire, part of the first city wall, back to boulevard Anspach and cross over into rue de l'Evêque to place de la Monnaie with the Théâtre de la Monnaie. Take a right into rue des Fripiers and left into rue Grétry, which becomes rue des Bouchers, where Janneken Pis is signposted.

LESSER-KNOWN BRUGES

Leave the Markt along Philipstockstraat, turn left into Cordoeaniersstraat to St-Jansplein. On the other side take St-Jansstraat to St-Maartensplein, with the baroque church of Sint-Walburgakerk. Walk along the left side of the church in Hoornstraat to the Verversdijk, then turn right and cross over the bridge to meet St-Annakerkstraat, with the Church of St Anna, dating to the 17th century ⊠ St-Annakerkstraat ⏰ April–Sep only. At the

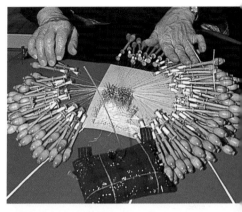

Lace making

back of the church, cross Jeruzalemstraat towards the Jeruzalemkerk on the corner. Next door is the Kantcentrum ⊠ Peperstraat 3, where you can see how lace is made.

From the Jeruzalemkerk turn into Balstraat and then Rolweg, with the Museum voor Volkskunde. Cross Rolweg to Carmersstraat and turn right. No. 85 is the striking dome of the Engels Klooster, the English convent, No. 174 the old Schuttersgilde Sint-Sebastiaan, the archers' guildhouse, and straight ahead on Kruisvest is the Sint-Janshuysmolen windmill. Take a right along Kruisvest. On the corner with Rolweg is a museum dedicated to the Flemish poet Guido Gezelle (1830–99) and further along, the Bonne Chiere windmill. At Kruispoort, turn right into Langestraat. At No. 47 is the Brewery Museum ⊠ Verbrand Nieuwland, 10 ☎ 33 06 99 ⏰ Jun–Sep: Wed–Sun 2–5. Before the end of Langestraat, turn left over a bridge onto Predikherenstraat, cross another bridge and turn right to Groenerei, one of Bruges' loveliest corners. At the end of the street is Vismarkt, with a fish market (Tuesday to Saturday mornings). To the right an alley under the arch leads to the Burg.

THE SIGHTS

- ● Markt (➤ 46)
- ● Sint-Walburgakerk (➤ 53)
- ● Sint-Annakerk
- ● Jeruzalemkerk (➤ 53)
- ● Voor Volkskunde (➤ 51)
- ● Engels Klooster
- ● Windmills (➤ 39), (➤ 55)
- ● Kruispoort (➤ 39)
- ● Brewery Museum
- ● Groenerei (➤ 59)
- ● Vismarkt
- ● Burg (➤ 47)

INFORMATION

Distance 3km
Time 2–3 hours
Start point Markt
🚌 bIII
🚊 1, 2, 3, 4, 8, 11, 13, 17
End point Burg
🚌 bIII
🚊 1, 2, 3, 4, 8, 11, 13, 17

EVENING STROLLS

Choosing a restaurant

A BAR TOUR OF BRUSSELS

Start with a typical Brussels' apéritif – *half en half*, half champagne and half white wine – at the Metropole Hotel (➤ 85) on the place de Brouckère. Exit to the right and after 20m turn right into the Passage du Nord. Turn right again at the end of the passage into rue Neuve heading towards the place la Monnaie to try the house beer in La Lunette (➤ 68). Turn right off the *place* into rue du Fossé aux Loups, where No. 29 is the Café Old Paris, a real 'brown' café (traditionally a bar where alcohol is served) and turn right again past the SAS Radisson Hotel opposite the famous bar A La Mort Subite (➤ 68). Walk through Galeries St.-Hubert, taking the first passage to the right into rue des Bouchers, then the first left past the Théâtre de Toone (➤ 81). Walk towards the Marché aux Herbes and into the Grand' Place, then turn right into rue au Beurre. The Falstaff terrace is to the left of the Bourse, to the right is the Cirio, with a cross-section of Brussels.

BRUGES BY NIGHT

From the Markt walk along Steenstraat to Simon Stevinplein, turn left into Mariastraat, and at the end of the street view the tower of the Onze-Lieve-Vrouwekerk (➤ 43) and the Gruuthuse Museum courtyard (➤ 44). Walk along the Dijver and cross over into Rozenhoedkaai; take the first passage left to Huidenvettersplein. Walk past the Vismarkt and along to the romantic Steenhouwersdijk (Groenerei). Cross the bridge to the left into Meestraat and then left into Hoogstraat, which ends at the Burg (➤ 47).

INFORMATION

A Bar Tour of Brussels
Distance 1km
Time a few hours depending on the number of stops
Start point place de Brouckère
🚇 E7
🚇 De Brouckère,
End point Bourse
🚇 E7
🚌 Tram 23, 52, 55, 56, 81

Bruges by night
Distance 1km
Time 1 hour
Start point Markt
🚇 bIII
🚌 All buses
End point Burg
🚇 bIII
🚌 All buses

Organised Sightseeing

BRUSSELS

ARAU (Atelier de recherche et d'Action Urbaines)
Brussels 1900, a bus tour, shows art-nouveau architecture and visits Horta buildings seldom open to the public ✉ 55 boulevard Adolphe Max/Adolphe Maxlaan ☎ 219 3345 ⏰ Mar–Nov: Sat.

Brukselbinnenstebuiten Guided coach tours and walks focus on Brussels' hidden corners by day and after dark ✉ 16 rue Vieux Marché-aux-Grains, box 1 ☎ 511 7883.

Brussels City Tours These start with a guided walk on the Grand' Place, followed by a bus ride to Brussels' main sights (3 hours) ✉ 8 De Boeck, rue de la Colline (Grand' Place) ☎ 513 7744.

Chatterbus Tours are in several languages including English, and by bus, on public transport or on foot ✉ 12 rue des Thuyas ☎ 673 183, fax 675 1967.

Other ways to discover Brussels

The old-fashioned way to tour the centre is by horse-drawn cab from the rue Charles Buls near the Grand' Place (☎ 053 70 05 04). The Brussels waterways can be discovered on a boat cruise organised by Brussels by Water (✉ 2 bis quai des Péniches ☎ 203 6406). Hélitan offers helicopter flights over Brussels (✉ 40 avenue J. Wybian ☎ 361 2121).

BRUGES

Bruges by Boat Explore the city by taking a 32-minute boat trip on the canals (➤ 59). Trips start from the Dijver, Katelijnestraat, Wollestraat, Huidenvettersplein and Vismarkt. ⏰ Mar–Nov: daily 10–6. Dec weekends only. Closed Jan.

Bruges by Bike Quasimodo offer a variety of guided bicycle tours of the main and lesser-known sights. They also organize longer cycling tours to Damme, the surrounding countryside and as far as the Dutch border ☎ 37 04 70 ⏰ mid-Mar–Oct: daily 10AM

Horse-drawn cabs Attractive ride touring the historic centre leaves from the Burg (35 minutes). Possible queues in summer ⏰ mid-Mar–Nov: daily 10–6.

City Tour Brugge A coach leaves the Markt hourly for a 50-minute tour of Bruges' historic sights. Tours in several languages including English ⏰ All year. Daily from 10AM.

busstop: markt - every hour

EXCURSIONS

Waterloo: the battlefield. Inset: statue topping the Butte de Lion

FROM BRUSSELS

WATERLOO

Just 20km south of Brussels is the famous battlefield where on 18 June, 1815, the Duke of Wellington defeated Napoleon Bonaparte. The Butte de Lion, a grass-covered pyramid erected by the Dutch a decade later to mark the spot where William of Orange was wounded, is what most people come for, and few are disappointed. At the foot of the mound is the visitor centre with a Waterloo panorama. It is well worth climbing the 226 steps for the views from the top. The Wellington Museum ☎ 02 354 7806, in the inn where the Duke was lodged, shows memorabilia from the battle, including an officer's wooden leg. The Museum of Caillou ☎ 02 384 2424, in a farm where Napoleon spent the night, also displays a few battlefield souvenirs.

LEUVEN

Leuven is a pleasant Flemish university town. The 15th-century Stadhuis (Town Hall) on the Grote Markt is typical of late Brabant Gothic style, while the Tafelrond is a neo-Gothic reconstruction of 15th-century houses. St Peter's Church has two wonderful triptychs by the 15th-century painter Dirk Bouts. The grandest of all the cafés around the Grote Markt is Café Gambrinus, which has pre-art nouveau frescos. Nearby is St-Michielskerk, a marvel of 17th-century baroque, while the Groot Beginhof is a village in itself with 17th- and 18th-century houses, now part of Belgium's largest university, the Catholic University of Leuven. Quiet in June, when students are taking their exams, the town bounces back to life in July and August.

FROM BRUGES

DAMME

When the old port in Bruges dried out after the estuary silted up at the end of the 15th century, the focus of trade shifted to Damme, a small, pleasant town only 6.5km from Bruges. Today it is a popular excursion by foot,

Damme windmill

bike or boat, with culinary delights at the end: restaurants and tea rooms offer local specialities such as *anguilles au vert* (river eel in herb sauce), Damme sausages, Damme tart and a semi-hard Damme cheese. On the main square stands the 19th-century statue of Jacob van Maerlant (1235–1300), the Flemish poet who wrote his best work in Damme. The elegant Gothic Stadhuis (Town Hall) of 1464 has two punishment stones on the corner and some fine mouldings inside the Council Hall and the Vierschaere. The Church of Our Lady dates back to the 14th century, but the aisles, nave and transept were pulled down in 1725. From the top of its 45-m high tower there are magnificent views over town and country. The 6.5–8km towpath by the canal from Bruges to Damme is perfect for an afternoon walk.

KNOKKE

Close to the Dutch border, Knokke is Belgium's most elegant seaside resort, its quiet green lanes lined with turn-of-the-century villas and small hotels. Brussels and Antwerp bourgeoisie come to the chic Het Zoute neighbourhood in summer and on weekends to browse in some of Belgium's smartest boutiques and jewellers, and in the many art galleries. The beaches are clean and get wider as you go toward Holland. The Zwin nature reserve is great for bird-watchers.

INFORMATION

Damme

Distance 6.5km

Journey time Bus 15 minutes, boat 35 minutes

🚌 799 from Bruges station

🚢 The *Lamme Goedzak* runs Apr–Sep

　📧 Noorweegse Kaai 31

　☎ reservations: 35 33 19

　🕐 from Bruges 10, 12, 2, 4:20 and 6; from Damme 9:15, 11, 1, 3, 5:20

🛈 Huyse de Grote Sterre, Jakob van Maerlanstraat 3, Damme

　☎ 050 35 33 19

Knokke

Distance 20km

Journey time 25 minutes by train

🚆 Frequent trains to Knokke

🚌 788/1 from Bruges station or t'Zand

🛈 Zeedijk-Knokke 660

　☎ 050 63 03 80

WHAT'S ON

Brussels' daily newspapers have listings of what's on. *The Bulletin*, the only English-language weekly devoted to business and EU matters, has a 'What's On' supplement with good listings. *Humo* has listings in Flemish, and *Kiosk* covers nightlife, concerts and exhibitions in French. Tickets are usually available at the appropriate venues, but can also be purchased from the Tourist Information Brussels (TIB) ✉ Grand' Place ☎ 513 8940 or FNAC (bookshop and ticket agency) ✉ City2 rue Neuve ☎ 209 2211. In Bruges, the monthly *Exit* magazine, available free at the tourist office, includes a detailed calendar of events.

January	*Brussels International Film Festival.*
February	*Binche Carnival* in Brussels (mid-February).
April–May	Brussels royal greenhouses (Serres Royales) open to the public (► 55).
May	*Procession of the Holy Blood*, or Ascension Day, in Bruges (► 60).
	Brussels Jazz Marathon (end of the month): There are jazz concerts on the Grand' Place and in 60 bars.
	Brussels: 20-km run past sights (last Sunday).
	Summer Festival. Good classical concerts in Brussels (May/June–September).
June	Re-enactment of the Battle of Waterloo at Waterloo ☎ 354 9910 (mid-June, every five years; next event due 2001).
July	*Brussels Ommegang* (first week ► 60).
	Cactus Festival in Bruges (second weekend). Open-air concerts in Minnewater Park, Bruges.
	Foire du Midi (mid-July to mid-August). Largest fair in Europe with over 1.5km of attractions and kiosks selling food in Brussels.
	National Day festivities in Brussels (21 July).
August	Raising of the *Meiboom*, or maypole, in Brussels (9 August ► 60).
	Floral carpet (mid-August on even-numbered years). On Brussels' Grand' Place.
	Reiefeesten or Festival of the Canals (every three years; next in 2002). Walk along Bruges' canals to see historical *tableaux vivants* at the monuments.
September	*Gouden Boomstoet*, or Pageant of the Golden Tree (every five years ► 60) in Bruges.
	Heritage Days: Hundreds of houses and monuments open their doors to the public throughout Belgium.
October–December	*Europalia* arts and cultural events in Brussels.

BRUSSELS' & BRUGES'
top 25 sights

The sights are shown on the maps on the inside front cover and the inside back cover and are numbered **1–25** *from west to east across the cities*

LA BASILIQUE DE KOEKELBERG

DID YOU KNOW?

- Koekelberg is dedicated to the nation's martyrs
- 44,000 Belgians died in World War I
- 700,000 more were deported to Germany
- Most Belgians are Catholic but in the 16th century many became Lutherans and Calvinists
- Under the Edict of Blood, up to 30,000 people were executed

INFORMATION

- C5
- 1 parvis de la Basilique,
- 425 8822
- Easter–Oct 31: Mon–Sat 9–5. Nov 1–Easter: Mon–Sat 10–4
- None
- Simonis and tram 19
- 87, AL, 49, 355
- Few
- Free (guided tours moderate)
- Guided tours of dome Mon–Fri 11 and 3; Sat, Sun 2 and 5:45

Approaching Brussels from the north or west, you will see a dramatic domed building. The National Basilica of Koekelberg, intended as a symbol of unification, impresses by its sheer size.

The building Koekelberg, more properly known as the Basilique Nationale de Sacré Coeur, is the world's largest art-deco-style church, a fitting monument to the Sacred Heart and to the nation's martyrs, to whom it is dedicated. Construction began in 1935 and continued until 1979. The enormous building, 167m by 89m with a soaring dome 22m in diameter can seem cold and gloomy on a dull day, but the scale of the choir is impressive and there are ten interesting chapels in the transepts on either side of the altar, representing the nine provinces of Belgium and the Belgian Congo. Stained-glass windows from the 1930s and 1940s are labelled. The statue of Our Lady, the Regina Paci, is to the left of the altar of the Sacré Coeur (Sacred Heart), and is worth seeking out. There are breathtaking views over Brussels and its environs from the outside gallery right under the dome.

Its significance The national monument dedicated to the memory of compatriots, Koekelberg is often seen as a symbol of the country's somewhat uneasy unification of French and Flemish cultures. Although the Pope is known for kissing the ground on arrival in a country, he was unable to do so at Brussels airport for fear of being seen to show favour to the Flemish, in whose territory the airport lies. It was not until he reached Koekelberg that he dared to bend down and kiss the ground. However, even here the divisions in the community are evident – there are separate services in French and Flemish.

2

HEYSEL

To celebrate Belgium's 100th birthday in 1930, the Heysel Park was named as the site of the Centenary Stadium and the Palais du Centenaire. To many the park also recalls a sombre episode in football history.

The Atomium The Atomium was designed in steel and aluminum for Expo '58 by Andre Waterkeyn. Its nine balls represent the atoms of a metal crystal enlarged 165 billion times. Inside, an exhibition covers the history of medicine, laboratories, virology, cells and genetics – dull, perhaps, but the panoramic view from the top of the atoms is spectacular.

Stranger landmarks After the Universal Exhibition in Paris in 1900, King Leopold II wanted his own chinoiseries, so he commissioned Parisian architect Alexandre Marcel to create them. The striking Japanese Tower, the former Entrance Pavilion to the Japanese Pagoda from the Paris Exhibition, was brought to Brussels. The splendid Chinese Pavilion, whose façade was carved in Shanghai, houses a fine collection of porcelain from the late 17th to the early 19th centuries. Both pavilions are in beautiful woodlands.

Trade space The Centenary Stadium hosts major rock concerts and sports events (and in 1985 was the site of an unfortunate and tragic football match when many fans were trampled, killing 39 people). Also in art-deco style, the Palais de Centenaire forms the core of the Trade Mart, whose ten exhibition halls make the city a unique venue for trade fairs in Europe.

HIGHLIGHTS

- The Atomium
- Japanese Tower
- Chinese Pavilion

INFORMATION

- ✚ Atomium D2 ✉ boulevard du Centenaire ☎ 474 8977
  🕐 Apr–Aug: daily 9–8. Sep–Mar: daily 10–6
  🍴 Restaurant Mon–Sat
  🚌 84, 89; tram 23, 81
  💰 Expensive
- ✚ Japanese Tower & Chinese Pavilion F2 ✉ 44 avenue van Praet ☎ 268 1608
  🕐 Tue– Sun 10–4:40
  🚌 53; tram 19, 23, 52
  💰 Moderate
- 🚫 Closed hols
- Ⓜ Heysel/Heizel
- ♿ None
- ↔ Bruparck (▶ 56), parc de Laeken (▶ 57)

*Top: the Atomium.
Left: the Japanese
Tower*

LES MAROLLES

DID YOU KNOW?

- Pieter Bruegel, born 1525, lived at 152 rue Haute

INFORMATION

- ✚ E8
- ✉ The area around place du Jeu de Balle
- 🍴 Restaurants nearby
- 🚇 Porte de Hal/Halleepoort
- 🚌 20, 48; tram 91
- ♿ Few
- ↔ Le Sablon (➤ 30), avenue Louise (➤ 35), Église Notre-Dame-de-la-Chapelle (➤ 53), Palais de Justice(➤ 55)
- ❓ Junk market 7AM–2PM

Top: junk market in the place du Jeu de Balle

Dwarfed by the Palais de Justice and hemmed in by the luxurious and graceful Sablon quarter, the neighbourhood of the Marolles is a reminder of working-class Brussels, with its narrow cobbled streets and many antique shops.

The heart and soul of Brussels Developed in the 17th century as a residential area for craftsmen working on the palaces and grand houses of the Upper City, the Marolles remained a lively working-class area until the 1870s, when the River Senne was covered and many artisans moved farther out. In the 19th century, part of the Marolles was demolished to make way for the imposing Palais de Justice. In the shadow of this symbol of law and order, the district became a crumbling haven for the city's poor and for Maghrebi immigrants from northwest Africa.

Where to go The Marolles stretches roughly from the Porte de Hal to the Église Notre-Dame-de-la-Chapelle; rue Blaes and the rue Haute are its main thoroughfares. The streets around the place du Jeu de Balle are full of snack bars, smoky traditional cafés, and junk shops. The junk market, held on the place du Jeu de Balle, is the place to look for unusual objects at bargain prices, especially on Sunday mornings, the market's liveliest time.

Property speculation The Marolles is changing quickly as property speculators, art galleries, and the fashionable crowd move in. Neither the indigenous inhabitants nor new immigrant families have the money to save their homes from the wrecker's ball, but action groups are working for the preservation of the Marolles and the restoration of its buildings.

MANNEKEN PIS

If it were not for the bus loads of tourists who gather in front of this little fellow to have their picture taken, it might be easy to miss him – a strange mascot for a city.

The cheeky cherub Manneken Pis, meaning literally 'the pissing little boy', is one of Brussels' more amusing symbols. The tiny bronze statuette, less than 60cm high, was created by Jérôme Duquesnoy the Elder in 1619. Known then as 'Petit Julien', it has since become a legend. One story claims that the Julien on whom the statue was modelled was the son of Duke Gottfried of Lorraine; another alleges that the statue urinated on a bomb fuse to save the Town Hall from destruction.

Often vandalised The statue was kidnapped by the English in 1745, as a way of getting at the people of Brussels, and two years later the French took him away. In 1817 he was stolen by a French convict and was in pieces when he was recovered. Those fragments were used to make the mould for the present statue. Even now he remains a temptation: he has been removed several times by drunk or angry students.

An extravagant wardrobe The French king Louis XV gave him a richly embroidered robe and the cross of Louis XIV as reparation for the bad behaviour of his soldiers in 1747. By now, Manneken Pis has hundreds of costumes, which you can see in the Musée de la Ville de Bruxelles (➤ 50–51).

DID YOU KNOW?

- In 1985 feminists demanded a female version of Manneken Pis and commissioned Janneken Pis (✉ Impasse de la Fidelité off the Rue des Bouchers)
- Every September 13 Manneken Pis wears the uniform of a sergeant in the Regiment of Welsh Guards to celebrate the liberation of Brussels in 1944

INFORMATION

- ✚ E7
- ✉ Corner of rue de l'Etuve and rue du Chênet
- ⊚ Gare Centrale/Centraal Station or Bourse/Beurs
- ▣ Tram 23, 52, 55, 56, 81
- 🎟 Free
- ↔ Grand' Place (➤ 28), Hôtel de Ville (➤ 29), Musée de la Costume et de la Dentelle (➤ 50), Musée de la Ville de Bruxelles (➤ 50–51)
- ❓ See sign at the statue for the dates when it is dressed up

Top and left: two of Manneken Pis's luxurious costumes

BRUSSELS

GRAND' PLACE

HIGHLIGHTS

- Hôtel de Ville
- La Maison du Roi, now the Musée de la Ville de Bruxelles
- Elegant dome of Roi d'Espagne
- Bronze plaques of Charles Buls and Everard 't Serclaes in arcade to left of Hôtel de Ville, which can be stroked for good luck
- Floral arrangement carpets the square, Aug in even-numbered years

INFORMATION

- E7
- Restaurants nearby
- Gare Centrale/Centraal Station or Bourse/Beurs
- Tram 23, 52, 55, 56, 81
- Good
- Free
- Manneken Pis (➤ 27), Centre Belge de la Bande Dessinée (➤ 37), Musée de la Ville de Bruxelles (➤ 50–51), Musée de Costume et de la Dentelle (➤ 50)
- Daily flower market; bird market on Sun; mid-Dec Christmas fair with Christmas tree, live animals, shopping, food, concerts

In the morning, the early sun lights up the gilded Gothic, Renaissance and baroque façades of one of the world's most stunning squares. The Grand' Place is the unquestionable heart of Brussels.

The centre of Brussels The Grand' Place is still the sight that all tourists come to admire. By the 11th century the market place was already humming and by the 13th century organisations of tradesmen known as guilds grew up to regulate working conditions and hours as well as trading outside the town. In the 13th century the three first guild halls, for butchers, bakers and clothmakers, were built in the Grand' Place. From then on the guilds' power increased; they became involved in wars, including the Battle of the Golden Spurs (1302), and commanded ever higher membership fees. The guilds' might is never more palpable than when you stand in the Grand' Place. Almost totally destroyed by a French bombardment in 1695, the square was entirely rebuilt by the guilds in less than five years.

The guildhalls Each one in the Grand' Place is distinguished by distinct statues and ornate carvings. Look for No. 5 La Louve (the She-wolf), representing the archers' guild; No. 7 Le Renard (Fox), the haberdashers' guild; No. 9 Le Cygne (Swan), the butchers' guild, where Karl Marx and Friedrich Engels wrote the *Communist Manifesto* in 1848; Nos. 24–5 La Chaloupe d'Or (Golden Galleon), the tailors' guild; and No. 26–7 Le Pigeon, representing the painters' guild, where novelist Victor Hugo stayed in 1852. Of particular interest are Nos. 29–3, the Maison du Roi, also called the Broodhuis in Flemish; it belonged not to a king but to the bakers' guild.

HÔTEL DE VILLE

Had architect Jan von Ruysbroeck forseen how much his elegant bell tower for the Hôtel de Ville would be admired today, perhaps he would not have thrown himself off it.

A Gothic masterpiece Flanders and Brabant have a wealth of Gothic town halls, but the Brussels Hôtel de Ville is probably the most beautiful of all. It was started in the spring of 1402; the right wing was added in 1444. The 96-m high octagonal tower, added later by architect Jan van Ruysbroeck, bears a gilt statue of the Archangel St Michael. The top of the tower, 400 steps up, gives the best views over the Grand' Place and the heart of Brussels. Most sculptures adorning the façade of the Town Hall are 19th-century replacements of 14th- and 15th-century originals that are now in the Musée de la Ville de Bruxelles (►50–51). The courtyard has two 18th-century fountains against the west wall, representing Belgium's most important rivers – the Meuse (to the left) and Scheldt (on the right).

The Grand Staircase The Grand Staircase carries the busts of all the mayors of Brussels since Belgian independence in 1830. Count Jacques Lalaing painted the murals on the walls in 1893.

The Gothic Hall The former 16th-century Council Chamber was used for official ceremonies. The lavish 19th-century tapestries are interesting for their depiction of the city's main guilds and their crafts. The windows are decorated with the coats of arms of Brussels' guilds and noble families. The official guided tour also includes some of the offices of the mayors and magistrates.

Top: town hall façade
Above: St. Michael

HIGHLIGHTS

- Grand Staircase
- bell tower
- magnificent tapestries

INFORMATION

- E7
- Grand' Place
- In tourist office: 279 4365
- Guided tours only, in English, (check with tourist office for times); groups Thu only
- Gar Centrale/Centraal Station or Bourse/Beurse
- Tram 23, 52, 55, 56, 81
- Good
- Moderate
- Museé de la Ville de Bruxelles (►50–51)
  Mannekin Pis (►27)

29

7

LE SABLON

HIGHLIGHTS

- Église de Notre Dame du Sablon
- Statues on the place du Petit Sablon
- Antiques market and shops
- Garden behind Palais d'Egmont
- Patisserie Wittamer

Top: the antiques market
Above: chocolates

INFORMATION

- ✚ E8–F8
- ☎ Church: 511 5741
- 🕐 Church: Mon–Fri 8–6; Sat 9:30–6; Sun 10–6
- 🍽 Restaurants, cafés and tearooms nearby
- 🚌 20, 48; tram 91, 92, 93, 94
- ♿ Good
- ↔ Les Marolles (► 26), Musées d'Art Ancien et Moderne (► 32, 33), place Royale (► 34)
- ❓ Antiques market Sat 9–6; Sun 9–2 (► 58); *Ommegang* procession (► 60)

The Sablon, the neighbourhood with the Grand and Petit Sablon squares at its centre, is a favourite destination for antique dealers. It is also perfect for strolling and its terraces are lovely places to sit and watch the world go by.

La place du Grand Sablon Many of Brussels' 17th-century aristocracy and bourgeoisie lived in this elegant square, which is now the centre of the antiques trade and the site of many specialist food shops. The Patisserie Wittamer (► 74) sells wonderful cakes and hand-made chocolates.

La place du Petit Sablon Mayor Charles Buls commissioned this square in 1890. The statue of the Counts of Egmont and Horne, beheaded by the Duke of Alba because of their religion, was moved here from the Grand' Place and is surrounded by statues of famous 16th-century scholars and humanists. Behind the garden, the 16th-century Palais d'Egmont, rebuilt in the early 20th century after a fire, is used for receptions by the Ministry of Foreign Affairs.

Église de Notre Dame du Sablon The 15th-century church of Notre Dame du Sablon is a fine example of flamboyant Gothic architecture, built over an earlier chapel with a miraculous statue of the Virgin Mary. A hemp weaver from Antwerp heard celestial voices telling her to steal the Madonna statue at the church where she worshipped and take it to Brussels. The choir and the stained-glass windows are particularly beautiful. Many statues, pinnacles, turrets and parts of the façade were finished or restored in 19th-century neo-Gothic style.

MUSÉE DE VICTOR HORTA

Many of the grand buildings designed by art-nouveau architect Victor Horta have been destroyed, but here in his house in the rue Américaine, the flowing lines and the play of light and space clarify his vision.

The house and workspace Victor Horta (1861–1947) built these two houses on the rue Américaine as his home and studio between 1898 and 1901. Now a museum, they clearly illustrate the break he made from traditional town houses, with their large, sombre rooms. Horta's are spacious and airy, full of mirrors, white tiles and stained-glass windows. A light shaft in the middle of the house illuminates a banister so gracious and flowing that you just want to slide down it. The attention to detail in the house is amazing, even down to the last door handle, all designed in fluid art-nouveau style.

Art nouveau in St-Gilles Although only Horta's house is open to the public, wealthy residential St-Gilles still has many others. Wandering around the neighbourhood between the rue Defacqz and the prison of St-Gilles you can admire several examples of this art-nouveau style, which dates from the late 19th to early 20th centuries. Paul Hankar designed the Ciambarlani and Janssens mansions at Nos. 48 and 50 rue Defacqz, and his own house at No. 71. One of the most beautiful art-nouveau façades in Brussels, designed by Albert Roosenboom, is 85 rue Faider. At No. 83 rue de Livourne you can see the private house of the architect Octave Van Rysselberghe, who also built the Otlet mansion at No. 48 rue de Livourne. The Hannon mansion, built at No. 1 avenue de la Jonction by Jules Brunfaut, is now a photographer's gallery; look for the impressive fresco by Paul-Albert Baudouin in the staircase.

DID YOU KNOW?

- Art nouveau originated in Britain in the 1880s but Brussels architects Paul Hankar, Henri van de Velde, and especially Victor Horta made it completely their own style
- ARAU trips visit other art-nouveau houses (➤ 19)
- The brochure 'Le Guide des décors céramiques à Bruxelles de 1880 à 1940' by Chantal Declève takes in 10 walks along the most beautiful art-nouveau façades in Brussels and is available from the tourist office on the Grand' Place, the Musée de Victor Horta, and good bookshops

INFORMATION

- ✚ E10
- ✉ 25 rue Américaine
- ☎ 543 0490
- ◷ Tue–Sun 2–5:30
- ▯ 54, 60; tram 81, 82, 91, 92
- ♿ Few
- ▮ Moderate Tue–Fri, expensive Sat, Sun

Top: art-nouveau staircase in the Musée de Victor Horta

9

BRUSSELS

Musée d'Art Ancien

HIGHLIGHTS

- *Landscape with the Fall of Icarus* and *The Census at Bethlehem*, Bruegel
- *The Ascent to Calvary* and *The Martyrdom of St Lievin*, Rubens
- *Marat Murdered in his Bath*, Jacques-Louis David
- *Days of September*, Gustav Wappers
- *The Scandalised Masks*, James Ensor
- *The Temptation of St Antony*, School of Hieronymus Bosch

INFORMATION

- ✚ F8
- ✉ 3 rue de la Régence
- ☎ 508 3211
- 🕐 Tue–Sun 10–5
- 🍴 Cafeteria
- 🚇 Gare Centrale/Centraal Station or Parc/Park
- 🚌 20, 34, 38, 60, 71, 95, 96; tram 92, 93, 94
- ♿ Good
- 🎫 Free. Charge for exhibitions
- ↔ Le Sablon (➤ 30), Musée d'Art Moderne (➤ 33), place Royale (➤ 34)
- ❓ Regular exhibitions, music and readings (information from Friends of the Museum ☎ 511 4116)

This dull, grey building houses a collection of art that is incredibly rich, created between the 15th and the end of the 19th centuries. The Bruegel and Rubens collections alone are worth travelling to see.

Museum history The Classical Art Museum and the neighbouring Modern Art Museum were founded by Napoleon Bonaparte in 1801 as the Museum of Brussels. The Classical Art Museum is housed in a building constructed in 1874–80 by Leopold II's colonial architect, Alphonse Balat. It underwent complete modernisation in the 1980s and is now connected to the Museum of Modern Art by an underground passage.

Artistic riches The museum highlights how rich a period the 14th to 17th centuries were in Belgian art history, peaking with Hans Memling's marvellous canvases and the bizarre visions of Hieronymus Bosch. The museum's collection of the works of the Bruegels is world-class, second only to that in Vienna's Kunst-historisches Museum. Also shown are works by Rogier van der Weyden, Dirk Bouts, Hugo van der Goes and, among later artists, Jacob Jordaens and van Dyck.

18th–19th centuries The museum's lower level contains 19th-century works by Gustave Courbet and Auguste Rodin. The central Forum, on the first floor, is home to a collection of 19th-century sculptures, including works by Jan van Kessels and Rodin, while the rooms off it contain masterpieces of the Romantic and Classical movements, including paintings by Delacroix.

Sculpture garden The sculpture collection in the garden beside the museum is less well known, but is excellent and well-arranged.

MUSÉE D'ART MODERNE

This museum puts modern Belgian artists in their context, and many of them shine, even among the great European stars. It also stages important temporary exhibitions.

20th-century Belgians Belgian artists are often overlooked in favour of their European and American contemporaries, so it is tempting to see something symbolic about the architecture of the Modern Art Museum, whose collection is buried in a multi-level subterranean building adjoining the Classical Art Museum. But by the time you have walked through the galleries of visual art, arranged chronologically (except for sculpture), you will certainly be seeing the light.

Fauvists and Surrealists Belgian artists, in the early 20th century, were particularly interested in fauvism and surrealism. Fauvism is best represented here by the works of Rik Wouters, Auguste Oleffe and Léon Spilliaert. Surrealism followed, with its rejection of aesthetic values, growing out of post-World War I chaos. Belgians René Magritte and Paul Delvaux stand out as two stars of surrealism and the museum collection includes one of Magritte's most famous paintings *The Dominion of Light*. Among the foreign artists that are represented here are Max Ernst, Francis Picabia and Oskar Kokoshka.

Other movements The museum follows the history of visual art in Belgium through futurism, abstract art and the 1960s to the present. There is also a collection of important works by Henri Matisse, Raoul Dufy, Picasso, Girogio de Chirico, Marc Chagall and Dali, which helps to put the Belgian artists in a wider context.

HIGHLIGHTS

- *L'Empire des Lumières* and others, René Magritte
- *The Flautist* and *The Woman with the Yellow Necklace*, Rik Wouters
- *In August, 1909*, Auguste Oleffe
- *The Public Voice* and *Pygmalion*, Paul Delvaux

INFORMATION

- ✚ F7
- ✉ 1–2 place Royale
- ☎ 508 3211
- 🕐 Tue–Sun 10–5
- 🍴 Cafeteria
- 🚉 Gare Centrale/Centraal Station or Parc/Park
- 🚌 20, 34, 38, 54, 60, 71, 95, 96; tram 92, 93, 94
- ♿ Very good
- 💳 Free. Charge for special exhibitions
- ↔ Le Sablon (➤ 30), Musée d'Art Ancien (➤ 32), place Royale (➤ 34)
- ❓ Regular temporary exhibitions as well as readings and music (information from Friends of the Museum ☎ 511 4116)

Top: Irène Hamoir, *René Magritte 1936*

33

PLACE ROYALE

HIGHLIGHTS

- Place du Musée
- Palace of Charles de Lorraine
- Place des Palais
- Fountain in parc de Bruxelles

INFORMATION

F7–F8

Classical Art, Modern Art & Dynasty museums

7 place des Palais ☎ 502 2541 ⏰ Tue–Sun 10–6
♿ None 💶 Moderate

Église de St-Jacques-sur-Coudenberg

Place Royale ☎ 511 7836
⏰ Mon–Sat 10–5
♿ None 💶 Free

Palais du Roi

Place des Palais ☎ 551 2020 ⏰ Jul 31–Sep 30: daily 10:30–4:30 ♿ Good
💶 Free

Parc/Park

20, 34, 38, 54, 60, 71, 95, 96; tram 92, 93, 94

Le Sablon (➤ 30), Musées d'Art Ancien et Moderne (➤ 32, 33)

Top: interior of the Palais du Roi. Right: Godefroid de Bouillon and the church of St-Jacques-sur-Coudenberg

This elegant neoclassical square is anchored by some of Belgium's most powerful institutions: the Royal Palace, the Belgian Parliament and the Law Courts.

Symmetrical square The place Royale, built between 1774–80, was originally an enclosed rectangle made up of eight palaces joined by porticos. Among them is the Palace of Charles de Lorraine (1766), the lovely neo-classical building just off the square under which the Museum of Modern Art was built.

Buildings The addition of the rue de la Régence on one side and the rue Royale and the park on the other later made the square more accessible. In its centre stands the statue of Godefroid de Bouillon, who led the first crusade. The palaces now house public offices, the museums of Classical and Modern Art and the interesting Dynasty Museum (chronicling the story of the Belgian royal family since 1830). On the east is the Église de St-Jacques-sur-Coudenberg.

Palais du Roi and parc de Bruxelles Nearby is the place des Palais with the Palais du Roi, the King's official residence and the parc de Bruxelles at its centre. Along the rue Royale is Horta's Palais des Beaux-Arts (1928) and the Film Museum, and on the rue de la Loi, the Belgian Parliament, the Palais de la Nation. In the park, once the monarch's hunting grounds designed by Guimard in *c*1775, pleasant tree-lined avenues lead up to a central fountain.

12

AVENUE LOUISE

Once a showpiece of Belgian progress, avenue Louise is now one of the places to go to see ladies heading for the designer boutiques jostling with kids from the fast-food joints.

Imperial design It's not hard to detect the stamp of Leopold II on avenue Louise. The thoroughfare was laid out in 1864 and was named after his eldest daughter. Stretching for 2km, as wide as a Parisian boulevard and just about pencil-straight (except where it swerves to avoid the Abbaye de la Cambre, ▶ 52), it remains the link between central Brussels and the Bois de la Cambre, with its attractive park and lake, and the countryside beyond.

Shopping This is where Brussels bureaucrats come to spend their money; they crowd the many smart cafés spilling on to the pavements and part with many hundreds of francs in its shops. It is one of the main shopping streets in the city and is lined with big-name designer boutiques, interior designers, main showrooms, art galleries, hotels and restaurants. Near place Louise, not far from Leopold's Palais de Justice, café-lined alleys run off the avenue. Beyond place Stéphanie, the avenue widens, the buildings get higher, the traffic increases and shop prices climb. Head for the galleries, the most famous and interesting of which are the Galeries de la Toison d'Or (Golden Fleece Galleries) and Galerie Louise on the intersecting avenue de la Toison d'Or.

Horta here At 224 avenue Louise, Victor Horta designed the Hôtel Solvay (1894–98), along with its furniture and silverware. Look through the glass door to glimpse the interior. Rue du Bailli, off the avenue, leads to rue Américaine and the Musée de Victor Horta (▶ 31).

HIGHLIGHTS

- Hôtel Solvay
- Chanel and other boutiques
- Galeries de la Toison d'Or
- Abbaye de la Cambre

INFORMATION

- ✛ E8, F9–F10, G10
- ✉ Area around avenue Louise
- 🍴 Restaurants nearby
- Ⓜ Louise/Louiza
- 🚌 34, 54, 60; tram 91, 92, 93, 94
- ♿ Good
- ↔ Les Marolles (▶ 26), Le Sablon (▶ 30), Palais de Justice (▶ 55)

Top: window shopping in the avenue Louise

13

BRUSSELS

CATHÉDRALE ST-MICHEL ET STE-GUDULE

HIGHLIGHTS

- Stained-glass windows
- 17th-century tapestries by Jaspar Van der Borght
- Nave pillars representing the 12 apostles
- Baroque pulpit by Henri Verbruggen (1699)
- Tombs of Johann of Brabant and his wife Margaret of York
- Stained glass by a pupil of Rubens in the Chapel of Our Lady of Redemption

INFORMATION

- ✚ F7
- ✉ place St Gudule
- ☎ 217 8345
- 🕐 Daily 8–6
- 🍴 None
- 🚇 Gare Centrale/Centraal Station or Parc/Park
- ♿ Few
- 🎫 Free. Crypt inexpensive
- ↔ Grand' Place (➤ 28), place Royale (➤ 34), Centre Belge de la Band Dessinée (➤ 37), musées d'Art Ancien et Moderne (➤ 32, 33), Musée du Cinéma (➤ 82)
- ❓ Services: in French Sat 5:30, Sun 10, 11:30, 12:30; in Flemish Sat 4

With its mixture of styles and influences, the cathedral of St Michael and Ste Gudule, on a hill between the upper and lower parts of the city, expresses the city's ability to compromise and is a fitting venue for state occasions.

Growing power During the 12th and 13th centuries, a valuable trade route between Brussels and Germany began to develop. As a result of the wealth this brought, a cathedral was planned and the splendid building was completed in the early 16th century. Subsequently embellished and added to, the building is now 108m long by 50m wide, with twin 69-m high towers. Unfortunately it is now surrounded by busy roads and ugly modern developments.

Slow start The cathedral is a mixture of middle and late Gothic styles. The earlier Romano-Gothic elements, particularly the ambulatory and choir, fit happily with those from the Late Gothic period, which are in the nave and on the west façade. Restorations undertaken since 1983 have exposed elements of an earlier Romanesque church (founded 1047) on which the cathedral was built. The original crypt is worth a visit.

Dedications Although known as St Michael's and Ste Gudule's, after Brussels' patron saints, and known by the people of Brussels as merely Ste-Gudule, the cathedral was officially dedicated only to St Michael. A story tells that when the building became a cathedral, the Roman Catholic authorities admitted to knowing nothing about Gudule, an 8th-century lady of royal blood sainted for her piety, and omitted her name.

Top: one of the stained-glass windows in the cathedral's nave

CENTRE BELGE DE LA BANDE DESSINÉE

Captain Haddock: ' "Land Ho! Land Ho! Thundering typhoons! Land ... about time, too!' Tintin: 'Why? ... Are we out of fuel-oil?' Haddock: 'Worse than that! ... We're out of whisky!!' " – Hergé's The Adventures of Tintin: The Shooting Star

Comic strips and more comic strips Combining comic strips and art nouveau, this is one of Brussels' unusual delights. Although comic strips, or *bds* (*bandes dessinées*), were not invented in Belgium, Belgian artists took the form to new heights. The most famous of them is Hergé (Georges Rémi), with his 1929 creations Tintin and Milou (Snowy). The wonderful collection of comic strips is housed in a stunning early 1900s building by architect Victor Horta. It is very much part of Belgian culture and well worth a visit.

Hands-on entertainment The museum is on several floors and re-creates the worlds of cartoon heroes. The mezzanine houses an extensive archive, a cinema and an exhibition that explains how *bds* are made. On the first floor, sections are devoted to each of the great Belgian *bd* creators, with pages to admire as well as hands-on exhibits. The ground floor exhibits work by Victor Horta.

The Magazins Waucquez The museum is housed in a building that a merchant named Monsieur Waucquez commissioned Victor Horta to build as a fabrics shop. Opened in 1906 with plant-motif ironwork, a sweeping staircase and glass skylight, Magazins Waucquez closed in 1970, and the building was earmarked for demolition until a pressure group and royal support saved it.

DID YOU KNOW?

- Tintin books have been translated into 51 languages
- More than 200 million Tintin books have been sold worldwide
- Brussels has a Comic Strip Frescoes Route, with the most famous characters painted on facades in the centre of Brussels (map available from tourist office on Grand' Place)

INFORMATION

- ✚ F7
- ✉ 20 rue des Sables
- ☎ 219 1980
- 🕐 Tue–Sun 10–6. Closed Easter and some hols
- 🍴 Restaurant
- Ⓠ Botanique/Botaniek, Gare Centrale/Centraal station, Rogier/de Brouckère
- 🚌 38, 58, 61; tram 23, 52, 55, 56, 81, 90, 92, 93, 94;
- ♿ Good
- 💰 Expensive
- ↔ Grand' Place (► 28), Cathédrale St-Michel et Ste-Gudule (► 36)
- ❓ Reading room Tue–Thu 12–5; Fri 12–6; Sat, Sun 10–6 (included in entrance fee). Library same hours, ticket moderate

Left: Tintin's moon rocket

PARC DU CINQUANTENAIRE

*Top: Autoworld. Above:
the Arc de Triomphe*

*Built to celebrate 50 years of Belgian inde-
pendence, the park has all that you would
imagine in the way of grand buildings –
even its own Arc de Triomphe. It also has
some surprises in store.*

The most famous city park In 1880, as part of
the celebrations for the 50th anniversary of
Belgian Independence, Leopold II ordered
the building of the Palais du Cinquantenaire,
with two huge halls, to hold the National
Exhibition in the park. For the next 25 years,
the king dreamed about erecting an Arc
de Triomphe. It was finally built in 1905
by Charles Girault, architect of the Petit Palais
in Paris, with two colonnades added in 1918.

Remarkable monuments Several features here
recall important international fairs. An Arab-
inspired building, which housed a painted
panorama of Cairo in an 1897 fair, is now Brussels'
Grand Mosque. A small pavilion, known as
Horta's pavilion (1889), was erected on designs
by the architect to house the haut-relief of the
Human Passions, by the sculptor Jef Lambeaux;
it is now closed but you can peep in the window.

Grand but dusty museums One of the National
Exhibition halls now showcases Autoworld, a
prestigious collection of vintage cars, which spans
the period from 1886 until the 1970s. The Musée
Royal de l'Armée et d'Histoire Militaire, in the
other hall, incorporates an aviation museum with
planes displayed in a huge hangar and houses
armor and weapons from medieval times to the
present. The rich Musée Royal d'Art et
d'Histoire, in the south wing of the Palais du
Cinquantenaire, has artefacts from ancient civi-
lizations, Belgian archaeological discoveries, and
important European decorative arts and lace.

HIGHLIGHTS

- Vintage cars in Autoworld
- Arc de Triomphe
- Lace collection

INFORMATION

- H7–H8
- Main entrances rue de la Lo
  & avenue de Tervueren

Autoworld
- 736 4165 Apr–Oct:
  daily 10–6. Nov–Mar: daily
  10–5 Café Good
  Moderate

Army & Military History museum
- 737 781193 Tue–Sun
  9–12, 1–4:30 Café
  Poor Free

Museum of Art & History
- 741 7211 Tue–Sun
  9:30–5 Café Poor
  Moderate

- Mérode, Schuman
- 20, 28, 36, 61, 67, 80; tram
  81, 82

DE VESTEN EN POORTEN

To understand Bruges' layout, take a ride or walk around its walls, especially on the east side, where the gates, ramparts, windmills and canals give the impression of containing the city, as they have done for 600 years.

Fortified Bruges Bruges' original fortifications (de Vesten en Poorten) date back to AD 1000, but nothing survives of the six original bastion gates beyond an inscription on Blinde Ezelstraat marking the location of the south gate. Between 1297 and 1300, as the medieval city grew increasingly wealthy, new defences were built; of the seven new gates, four survive in the east – Kruispoort (Cross Gate, 1402), with a drawbridge, and Gentpoort (Ghent Gate, 14th century) with twin towers – and two in the west – Bruges' only two-way gate, Smedenpoort (Blacksmiths' Gate, 14th century), and Ezelpoort (Donkeys' Gate, rebuilt in the 17th and 18th centuries).

Blowing in the wind The ramparts that linked the gates on the east side were used as raised platforms for windmills. Of the 25 mills marked on a panorama of Bruges from 1562, only four stand along the canal between Kruispoort and Dampoort today, and all are of more recent date. The first mill when viewed coming from Kruispoort, Bonne Chiere (Good Show), was built in 1888 and reconstructed in 1911, but has never worked. The second mill, Sint-Janshuysmolen (St. John's House Mill), near the intersection of Kruisvest and Rolweg, was built by bakers in 1770 (▶ 55). The third mill, De Nieuwe Papegaai (New Parrot), a 1790 oil mill, was moved to Bruges from Beveren in 1970. A fourth mill, constructed in the mid-1990s, is near the Dampoort.

DID YOU KNOW?

- Stone statue of St Adrian (1448, remodeled 1956) on Gentpoort was originally carved by Jan van Cutsegem to ward off plague
- Smedenpoort's bronze skull (hung there in 1911) replaces the real skull of a traitor
- Of the 25 windmills known to have stood in Bruges in 1562, 23 still existed in the 19th century, but between 1863 and 1879, 20 of them were pulled down
- The 6.5-km long ramparts of Bruges were laid out as parks in the 19th century and are pleasant for walking, particularly the areas around Begijnenvest; Buiten Smedenvest and Kruisvest are among the most beautiful

Top: contained by canals. Below: the Gentpoort

KATHEDRAAL ST-SALVATOR

HIGHLIGHTS

- *Martyr's Death of St Hippolytus*, Dirk Bouts' triptych (1470–5)
- *Last Supper*, Pieter Pourbus
- 14th-century *Tanner's Panel*
- *The Mother of Sorrows*
- Baroque statue of God the Father
- Eekhoute Cross in shoemakers' chapel
- Eight tapestries by Jaspar van der Borght

INFORMATION

- ✚ blII
- ✉ Zuidzandstraat
- 🕐 Summer: daily 10–11, 2–5; Sun 3–5. Winter: Mon, Tue, Thur–Sat 2–5. Closed hols
- 🔲 1, 2, 3, 4, 5, 8, 9, 11, 13, 16
- ♿ Very good
- 🎟 Cathedral free, museum inexpensive
- ↔ Onze-Lieve-Vrouwekerk (➤ 43), Gruuthuse Museum (➤ 44), Markt (➤ 46)
- ❓ Important concerts and church services during public hols, check with tourist office

The Kathedraal St-Salvator, together with the belfry and the Onze-Lieve-Vrouwekerk (Church of Our Lady), towers above Bruges. The extraordinary artworks inside are a reminder of the cathedral's long and eventful history.

The cathedral A house of prayer existed in this location as early as the 9th century; it was dedicated to St Saviour and to St Eloi, who is believed to have founded an earlier wooden church here in 660. The present cathedral was built toward the end of the 13th century. This cathedral was damaged by fires on several occasions, and in 1798 many of its treasures were stolen by the French, who put the building and its contents up for auction the following year. However, wealthy Brugeans bought a lot back. The neo-Romanesque top was added to the remarkable tower in 1844–6 and the spire in 1871. The oldest sections of the tower of the present church date back to 1127.

Sculptures and tapestries The cathedral houses some splendid sculptures and wonderful church furniture. The large statue of God the Father (1682) by Arthur Quellinus is one of the best baroque sculptures in Bruges. The doors of the shoemakers' chapel, as well as the sculptures in the Cross chapel and the Peter and Paul chapel, are superb examples of late Gothic oak carving. Six of the eight 18th-century tapestries in the choir and transept, illustrating the life of Christ, were woven in Brussels.

Flemish art in the museum The museum displays most of the church's collection. There are several wonderful pieces of 15th-century Flemish art among the 120 or so paintings, and there are gold and silver artefacts, pottery and manuscripts.

Top: one of the Brussels tapestries in the cathedral

BEGIJNHOF

Many Flemish cities have kept their béguines, but the one in Bruges is undoubtedly one of the oldest and most picturesque, a place of exquisite silence and repose.

Our Lady of Good Will

Closed court Beginning in the 12th century pious women started to live in communities, spending their days praying, making lace, looking after the sick and old and sometimes taking monastic vows. They lived apart from the city in *béguinages* or closed courts, whose entrances were shut at night. The Bruges *béguinage* consists of a number of houses ranged around one such square. Since 1927 it has been occupied by Benedictine nuns, whose severe black-and-white habits are a reminder of those of the *béguines*. Several times a day the nuns walk to the church through the green garden at the side of the square. The square is particularly beautiful in early spring, when it is abloom with daffodils.

The church As in many other *béguinages*, the simple church (1605) is dedicated to St Elisabeth of Hungary, whose portrait hangs above the entrance. She also appears in a painting by Bruges master Lodewijk de Deyster (1656–1711). The most important work is the statue of Our Lady of Spermalie (*c*1240), the oldest statue of the Virgin in Bruges. On the left wall as you face the altar is a superb statue of Our Lady of Good Will. The remarkable alabaster sculpture of the Lamentation of Christ at the High Altar dates from the early 17th century.

A *béguine*'s house The tiny museum at the back of the church, a reconstruction of a 17th-century *béguine*'s house, complete with furniture and household goods, gives an idea of how the community used to live.

HIGHLIGHTS

* The square
* Statue of Our Lady of Spermalie
* *Béguine*'s house

INFORMATION

➕ blV
✉ Wijngaardplein
☎ 33 00 11
🕐 Church and *béguinage* daily 6–12, 2:30–6. *Béguine*'s house Dec–Feb: Wed, Thu, Sat, Sun 2:45–4:15; Fri 1:45–6. Mar, Oct, Nov: daily 10:30–12, 1:45–5. Apr–Sep: Mon–Sat 10–12, 1:45–5:30; Fri 1:45–5:30; Sun 10–12, 1:45–6
🚏 1, 2
♿ Good
💲 Free. Museum inexpensive
↔ Memling Museum (➤ 42)

41

St-Janshospitaal en Memling Museum

DID YOU KNOW?

- On the back of *The Mystical Marriage of St Catherine*, Memling painted the donors
- Jan Florein donated *The Adoration of the Magi*, and is shown kneeling on the left of the painting
- Adriaan Reins, friar of the hospital, is on the side panel of *The Lamentation of Christ*
- Maria Portal

INFORMATION

- ✚ blV
- ✉ Mariastraat 38
- ☎ 44 87 11
- ⏰ Apr–Sep: daily 9:30–5. Oct–Mar: Thur–Sun 9:30–12:30, 2–5
- 🍴 Restaurants nearby
- ♿ Very good
- 💰 Moderate
- ↔ Canals (► 59)

Madonna with apple, Memling 1487

Among the must-sees of Bruges are the Hans Memling works on show here, 15th-century landmarks in the history of art. It's a bonus that the building that houses them is also a gem.

The hospital St. John's, founded in the 12th century, is one of Europe's oldest hospices (medieval hospitals) and continued functioning until 1976, when medical care was moved to a new building. The Gothic Maria Portal (*c*1270) on Mariastraat is the original gate. Subsequent buildings include a tower, central ward, monastery, brewery, bathhouse, cemetery (all 14th century), St. Cornelius Chapel (mid-15th century) and a convent for the hospital's sisters (1539). The old wards are closed for restoration at press time, but the 17th-century dispensary, with exhibits of ancient remedies, is particularly interesting and the church is open.

The Memling masterpieces As St John's reputation as a hospital grew, so did its wealth. Its funds were invested, with inspiration, in the works of Hans Memling, a German painter who had settled in Bruges by 1465 and died one of its richest citizens in 1494. Four of the six works on display here were commissioned by St John's friars and sisters, the most famous and unusual being the *Ursula Shrine* (1489), a relic box in the shape of a church, gilded and painted with scenes from the life of St Ursula. The triptych *Mystical Marriage of St Catherine* (1479) was commissioned for the chapel's main altar, as were two smaller triptychs – *The Adoration of the Magi* (1479) and *The Lamentation of Christ* (1480). The diptych *Madonna with Child* (1487) and the portrait of *The Sibylla Sambetha* (1480) were moved here from the former St Julian's hospice in 1815.

ONZE-LIEVE-VROUWEKERK

Beneath the monumental brick tower in this Church of our Lady, the religious feeling is palpable, heightened by the aroma of incense, the magnificent sculptures and the stunning paintings all around you.

One of Bruges' seven wonders Although there was a chapel here about 1,000 years ago, the choir and façade on Mariastraat date from the 13th century and the aisles and superbly restored Paradise Porch date from the 14th and 15th centuries. The church's most striking feature is the 122-m high tower, begun in the 13th century.

Artworks The star attraction is the *Madonna and Child* by Michelangelo (1475–1564). Other sculptures include a rococo pulpit (1743) designed by the Bruges painter Jan Garemijn, some fine altars, and the Lanchals monument in the Lanchals chapel (both 15th century). The prayer balcony connected to the Gruuthuse mansion (► 44) enabled the lords of the Gruuthuse to attend services directly from home. The church contains some important 16th-century Flemish paintings, including works by Gerard David, Pieter Pourbus and Adriaan Isenbrandt. The valuable *Katte of Beversluys*, kept in the sacristy, weighs 3kg and is embellished with enamel and precious stones.

Mausoleums Both Charles the Bold, who died in 1477, and Mary of Burgundy, who died in 1482 after a hunting fall, are buried here in superb adjacent mausoleums moved to the Lanchals chapel in 1806 and returned here in 1979. Excavations revealed beautiful 16th-century frescos in other tombs and also the fact that Mary's remains were buried with the heart of her son Philip the Fair.

HIGHLIGHTS

- Brick tower
- Paradise Porch
- Mausoleums of Charles the Bold and Mary of Burgundy
- *Madonna and Child*, Michaelangelo
- *The Adoration of the Shepherds*, Pieter Poubus
- *Our Lady of the Seven Sorrows*, probably by Adriaan Isenbrandt
- *The Transfiguration of Mount Tabor*, Gerard David

INFORMATION

- ✚ blV
- ✉ Mariastraat
- 🕐 Church Mon–Sat 10–11:30, 2:30–5; Sun 2:30–5 (4:30 in winter). Mausoleums Sat 10–11:30, 2:30–4:30 (4 in winter)
- 🚇 1
- ♿ Very good
- 💰 Church free, mausoleums inexpensive
- ↔ Kathedraal St-Salvator (► 40), Begijnhof (► 41), Memling Museum (► 42), Gruuthuse Museum (► 44), Groeninge Museum (► 45)
- ❓ Weekend services: Sat 5 and 6:30PM, Sun 11AM

Mausoleum of Charles the Bold

GRUUTHUSE MUSEUM

HIGHLIGHTS

- Sculpture rooms
- Prayer balcony
- Gombault and Macée Tapestry series
- Lace collection
- Illuminated courtyard at night
- Smallest window in Bruges, seen from the Boniface Bridge
- Views from loggia over Reie, Boniface Bridge, and Onze-Lieve-Vrouwekerk

INFORMATION

- ✚ blll
- ✉ Dijver 17
- ☎ Gruuthuse Museum 44 87 62; Brangwyn Museum 44 87 63
- ⏰ Apr–Sep: Wed–Mon 9:30–5. Oct–Mar: Wed–Mon 9:30–12:30, 2–5.
- ▣ 1
- ♿ None
- 🎟 Moderate; Brangwyn Museum inexpensive
- ↔ Kathedraal St-Salvator (▶ 40), St-Janshospitaal en Memling Museum (▶ 42), Onze-Lieve-Vrouwekerk (▶ 43), Groeninge Museum (▶ 45)

The peaceful façade and courtyard of the Gruuthuse Palace transport you back to medieval times. And it is a delight to stroll around the adjacent Arentspark and watch boats pass under the Boniface Bridge, one of Bruges most romantic corners.

The palace of Gruuthuse Built in the late 15th century by humanist and arts lover Louis van Gruuthuse, this now houses the Gruuthuse Museum, a fascinating collection of antiques and applied arts, well laid out in a series of 22 numbered rooms. There are some fine sculptures, including an early 16th-century Gothic kneeling angel rendered in oak; the impressive *Christ, Man of Sorrows* (*c*1500), and the 15th century *Reading Madonna* by Adriaan van Wezel.

Brugean Tapestries Well-preserved 17th-century examples in the Tapestry Room represent the Seven Liberal Arts; and some fine baroque wool and silk counterparts in Room 8 have pastoral themes, including the very excellent comic-strip like tapestry the *Country Meal*. Rooms 18 and 19 hold a precious lace collection. Room 16 is the prayer room, in the form of a balcony, that looks down into the Onze-Lieve-Vrouwekerk (▶ 43). Together with the kitchen, it is the oldest part of the building.

Brangwyn Museum (Arents Huis) Next door is the Arents Huis, which houses four important collections donated by wealthy Belgians to the city of Bruges: pewter from the 18th to the 20th centuries; 18th- and 19th-century works of art, including exquisite china; a collection of mother-of-pearl; and the world's largest collection of paintings by Frank Brangwyn (1867–1956), a Bruges-born British painter who studied under William Morris.

A delicate ironwork sign outside refers to the brewhouse origins of the palace

22

BRUGES

GROENINGE MUSEUM

Jan van Eyck's serene Portrait of Margaretha van Eyck *and Gerard David's gruesome* The Judgement of Cambyses, *portraying a Bruges magistrate being skinned alive, are so arresting that it is easy to overlook the contemporary art here.*

The Flemish Primitives The 15th-century Flemish Primitives were so named in the 19th century to express a desire to recapture the pre-Renaissance simplicity in art. Room 1 shows works by van Eyck (c1390–1441), including the masterwork *Madonna with Canon Joris van der Paele* and the superb *Portrait of Margaretha van Eyck*, the painter's wife. Two important works by Hans Memling – the *Moreel Triptych* and two panels of *The Annunciation* – are also present. Also displayed here are works by Rogier van der Weyden, Hugo van der Goes and the last of the Flemish Primitives, Gerard David, including his *The Judgment of Cambyses* and the large triptych *The Baptism of Christ*. In Room 7 the 16th-century works of Pieter Pourbus illustrate the Italian influence on Flemish style. In Room 8 keep an eye out for the lovely baroque *Portrait of a Brugean Family* by Jacob van Oost (1601–71).

Modern Flemish masters Flemish impressionist Emile Claus (1849–1924) and Rik Wouters (1882–1916) are well represented. Also look for James Ensor's *Le Parc aux Oiselles* and works of Gust de Smet, Gustave van de Woestijne and Rik Slabbinck; works by Constant Permeke represent the best of Flemish expressionism. There are two paintings by Paul Delvaux and one by René Magritte. The last room shows works from the 1950s to the 1970s by Brugeans Luc Peire and Gilbert Swimberghe and Roger Raveel; it also contains a cabinet by art-nouveau artist Marcel Broodthaers (1924–75).

HIGHLIGHTS

- *Portrait of Margaretha van Eyck*, van Eyck
- *Moreel Triptych* and *Annunciation*, Hans Memling
- *Portrait of a Brugean Family*, Jacob van Oost
- *The Assault*, René Magritte

INFORMATION

- ✚ clll
- ✉ Dijver 12
- ☎ 44 87 50
- 🕐 Apr–Sep: Wed–Mon 9:30–5. Oct–Mar: 9:30–12:30, 2–5. Closed Tue all year round
- 🍴 Cafeteria
- 🚹 1
- ♿ Good
- 💶 Expensive
- ↔ Markt (► 46), canals (► 59)

Top: Portrait of a Brugean Family. *Below:* the Moreel Triptych

45

23

MARKT

The Belfry, emblematic of Bruges' medieval power and freedom, dominates the city's main square, the Markt (Market). The square is ringed with Gothic and neo-Gothic buildings, which symbolize the power of Bruges merchants over its aristocracy.

DID YOU KNOW?

- Brugse Metten (18 May 1302) massacre, when Flemish workers and citizens killed hundreds of occupying French soldiers
- Statue of Jan Breydel and Pieter de Coninck was unveiled three times
- Belfry tower is 83-m high, has 366 steps to top and leans southeast
- Tower has a four-octave carillon of 47 bells cast by Joris Dumery in 1748
- Combined weight of bells is 27 tons
- Carillon marks the quarter hour

INFORMATION

- ✚ bill
- ✉ Markt
- ☎ 44 87 11
- 🕐 Belfry Apr–Sep: daily 9:30–5. Oct– Mar: daily 9:30–12:30, 1:30–5
- 🍴 Several restaurants and tea rooms nearby
- 🚌 1, 2, 3, 4, 5, 6, 7, 8, 9, 11, 13, 15, 16, 17, 25
- ♿ Good
- 🎫 Belfry tower moderate
- ↔ Kathedraal St Salvator (➤ 40), Burg (➤ 47), Basilica of the Holy Blood (➤ 48)
- ❓ Carillon concerts Oct–June 14: Wed, Sat, Sun 2:15–3PM. Jun 15–Sep: Mon, Wed, Sat 9–10PM; Sun 2:15–3PM

The historic square This square has always been at the heart of Bruges with its historic and attractive buildings. A weekly market was held here from 1200 onwards until it was moved to 't Zand in 1983. The late 19th-century neo-Gothic Provincial Government Palace and the Central Post Office (1887–1921) stand on the site of the former Waterhalles, a huge covered dock where ships moored. Across Sint-Amandstraat, is Craenenburgh House where Maximilian of Austria was locked up in 1488. The square's north side was once lined with tilers' and fishmongers' guildhalls, which are now restaurants. There is a bronze statue (1887) of two medieval Brugean heroes Jan Breydel and Pieter de Coninck, who in 1302 led the Brugse Metten, the massacre of hundreds of occupying French soldiers by Flemish workers. The same year saw the rebellion of the Flemish against the French king, Philip IV, at the Battle of the Golden Spurs, resulting in Flanders' independence.

The Halles and Belfry The origins of the Halles (town hall and treasury) and the Belfry (called 'Halletoren' in Bruges) go back to the 13th century, when the Halles were originally the seat of the municipality and the city's treasury. From the first-floor balcony, the bailiff read the 'Halles commands', while the bells warned citizens against approaching danger or enemies.

24

BURG

This historic enclave, with its many fine buildings, evokes medieval Bruges better than any other part of the city. The impressive structures once contained the offices of the city, county, church and judicial authorities.

A separate entity Until the 18th century, the Burg was walled in and locked with four gates. The north side of the square was dominated by the 10th-century St Donatian's Church, sold by auction and torn down soon after in 1799. (Under the trees, there is a scale model of the church, and some of its foundations can be seen in the basement of the Holiday Inn hotel.)

The square The whole of the square's west side was once the Steen, an impressive 11th-century tower; only the porch beside the stairs to the Basilica of the Holy Blood (➤ 48) remains. On the southeast side of the square, to the left of the Town Hall and across Blinde Ezelstraat, is the Flemish-Renaissance Civil Recorders' House (1535–7). On the eastern side of the square is the Palace of the Brugse Vrije (1722–7), a rural region along the coast that was subordinate to Bruges. The building, home to the Palace of Justice until the 1980s, now houses the tourist office and a museum containing the *Mantelpiece of Charles V*, a Renaissance work of art by Lancelot Blondeel.

The Town Hall Built between 1376 and 1420, Bruges' Town Hall is the oldest and one of the most beautiful in Belgium, with its turreted sandstone façade dating from 1376, though the statues on its Gothic façade date from the 1970s. The Gothic Room, with its superb ceiling, is where Philip the Good called together the first States General of the Ancient Low Countries in 1464; it is now reserved for private functions.

Above: detail of the Town Hall façade

HIGHLIGHTS

- Gothic Room in the Town Hall
- Town Hall façade
- Mantelpiece of Charles V in Brugse Vrije museum

INFORMATION

- ✚ blll
- ✉ Burg
- ☎ Tourist office 44 86 86
- ⚐ Town Hall (Gothic Room) Apr–Sep: daily 9:30–5. Oct–Mar: daily 9:30–12:30, 2–5. Museum Brugse Vrije Tue–Sun 10–12, 1:30–5
- 🍽 Restaurants nearby
- 🚌 All buses to the Markt
- ♿ Very good
- 💲 Inexpensive
- ↔ Markt (➤ 46), Basilica of the Holy Blood (➤ 48)
- ❓ Concerts in summer

47

HEILIG BLOEDBASILIEK

HIGHLIGHTS

- Reliquary of the Holy Blood
- *Virgin with Child*
- Bruges' oldest sculpture
- Painting of the *Legend of Saint Barbara* in the museum

INFORMATION

- ✚ bIII
- ✉ Burg 10
- 🕐 Apr–Sep: daily 9:30–12, 2–6. Oct–Mar: Thu–Tue 10–12, 2–4. Closed some hols and during services
- 🚌 All buses to the Markt
- ♿ None
- 💶 Inexpensive
- ↔ Markt (➤ 46), Burg (➤ 47), canals (➤ 59)
- ❓ Sun services 8AM–11AM. Worship of the Holy Blood Fri 8:30–11:45, 3–4. Ascension Day 8:30–10:15 and from 6PM

Top: Heilig Bloedkapel façade. Below: Heilig Bloed Procession, May

The Romanesque Chapel of the Holy Blood, shrouded in mystery, is rich with the atmosphere of the Middle Ages. Even travellers who are casual about their religion tend to fall silent in the face of the intense devotion of the worshippers here.

The Holy Blood Thierry of Alsace, Count of Flanders and a courageous crusader, is said to have received the relic with the blood of Jesus from the Patriarch of Jerusalem. He brought it to Bruges in 1150. Stored in two crystal vials, the relic is exhibited every Friday for adoration on the Blessing Altar in the Chapel of the Holy Blood, or the upper church. Although this area was originally Romanesque, it has been heavily restored in clumsy Gothic style. The original 15th-century stained-glass windows are now in London's Victoria & Albert Museum; those here are 19th-century copies.

The museum Contains paintings, silver, tapestries and the Reliquary of the Holy Blood. This gold and silver reliquary (1617) was made by Renaissance goldsmith Jan Crabbe and is decorated with pearls and precious stones. Each year it is carried around the city during the Procession of the Holy Blood (➤ 60).

St Basil's Chapel The lower chapel, a small Romanesque three-aisled church supported on thick sandstone columns, was built around 1139 on designs by Count Thierry of Alsace. It is dedicated to the Virgin Mary and to St Basil, the patron saint of bricklayers. The wooden *Virgin with Child* (*c*1300) is one of Bruges' most beautiful Gothic statues. The less refined 19th-century *Ecce Homo* in the side chapel is much adored. Bruges' oldest sculpture, a low-relief baptism (*c*1100), stands in the side-chapel passage.

BRUSSELS' & BRUGES' *best*

MUSEUMS

Musical instruments

How about Adolphe Sax, the inventor of the saxophone? A few saxophones are on show in the Sax Room of the Musée Instrumental (✉ 17 place du Petit Sablon ☎ 511 3595 🕐 Tue–Fri 9:30–4:45; Sat 10–4:45), one of the world's great collections of musical instruments, soon to move to the stunning Magasins Old England on the place Royale.

BRUSSELS

See Top 25 Sights for
CENTRE BELGE DE LA BANDE DESSINÉE (➤ 37)
MUSÉE D'ART ANCIEN (➤ 32)
MUSÉE D'ART MODERNE (➤ 33)
MUSÉE DE VICTOR HORTA (➤ 31)
MUSEUMS OF THE PARC DU CINQUANTENAIRE (➤ 38)

MUSÉE BRUXELLOIS DE LA GEUZE

The family-run Cantillon brewery, founded in 1900 and the last of the 50 independent breweries in Brussels that makes lambic (the typical beer of Brussels). It still produces beer in exactly the same way with the original equipment. Factory tours available.

➕ D7–D8 ✉ Brasserie Cantillon, 56 rue Gheude ☎ 521 4928 🕐 Mon–Fri 8:30–5; Sat 10–5, 🚇 Gare du Midi/Zuidstation, Clémenceau 🚌 20,47; tram 18, 23, 52, 55, 56, 81, 82, 90 ♿ Few 💷 Moderate, including beer

MUSÉE DE COSTUME ET DE LA DENTELLE

Here you will find a fine collection of old lace, embroidery and costumes; courses in lace-making; and interesting temporary exhibitions.

➕ E7 ✉ 6 rue de la Violette ☎ 512 7709 🕐 Apr–Sep: Mon, Tue, Thu, Fri 10–12:30 & 1:30–5; Sat–Sun 2–5:30; Oct–Mar: Mon, Tue, Thu, Fri 10–12:30 & 1:30–4; Sat–Sun 2–4 🚇 Gare Centrale/Centraal Station or Bourse/Beurs 🚌 29, 34, 38, 47, 48, 60, 63, 65, 66, 71, 95, 96; tram 23, 52, 55, 56, 81 ♿ Good 💷 Moderate

MUSÉE DE LA VILLE BRUXELLES

This 19th-century building, a careful reconstruction of the original Maison du Roi, is devoted to the city's history in all aspects, and displays a fine collection of paintings, tapestries, maps and manuscripts as well as the extensive wardrobe of Manneken Pis (➤ 27).

Below: Musée Royal de L'Afrique Centrale (Royal Museum for Central Africa)

➕ E7 ✉ Maison du Roi, Grand' Place ☎ 279 4350 🕐 Apr–Sept: Mon–Thu 10–12:30, 1:30–5. Oct–Mar: Mon–Thu 10–12:30, 1:30–4; Sat, Sun 10–1 all year 🚇 Bourse/Beurs, Gare Centrale/Centraal Station 🚌 29, 34, 47, 48, 60, 63, 65, 66, 71, 95, 96; tram 23, 52, 55, 56, 81 ♿ Few 💵 Moderate

MUSÉE ROYAL DE L'AFRIQUE CENTRALE

When it opened in 1897, the Royal Museum for Central Africa glorified the Belgian presence in Africa. Now, despite its grand façade, it is a musty place, popular with children for its dioramas with stuffed animals and for its large collection of creepy crawlies. The grounds are worth a visit – attractively laid out formal gardens, flanked by lakes and pleasant woods.

➕ Off map ✉ 13 Leuvensesteenweg, Tervuren ☎ 769 5211 🕐 Tue–Fri 10–5; weekends 10–6 🍴 Cafeteria 🚌 Tram 44 from metro station Montgommery ♿ Good 💵 Moderate

BRUGES

See Top 25 Sights for
GROENINGE MUSEUM (➤ 45)
GRUUTHUSE MUSEUM (➤ 44)
MEMLING MUSEUM (➤ 42)

MUSEUM ONZE-LIEVE-VROUW TER POTTERIE

A wonderful little museum in a former hospital (13th–17th centuries) that has been run as a nursing-home since the 15th century. There are sculptures, 15th and 16th-century paintings, tapestries and furniture. The church has one of Bruges' finest baroque interiors.

➕ cII ✉ Potterierei 79 ☎ 44 87 11 🕐 Apr–Sep: Thu–Tue 9:30–12:30, 1:15–5. Oct–Mar: Thu–Tue 9:30–12:30, 2–5 🚌 4 ♿ Very good 💵 Moderate

MUSEUM VOOR VOLKSKUNDE

Bruges' past is recalled in these 17th-century almshouses. Period rooms and exhibits explain the traditional professions, popular worship and costumes.

➕ cIII ✉ Rolweg 40 ☎ 44 87 11 🕐 Apr–Sep: daily 9:30–5. Oct–Mar: Wed–Mon 9:30–12:30, 2–5 🍴 Medieval inn In de Zwarte Kat 🚌 4, 6 ♿ Good 💵 Moderate

Above left: Ter Potterie Museum.
Below: Museum voor Volkskunde

51

CHURCHES

The Brussels *Béguinage*

The church of St John the Baptist, the finest example of Flemish baroque in the country, and the rue du Béguinage are all that are left of the once flourishing *Béguinage* founded in the 13th century outside the city walls. The former gardens were used to build the Hospice Pachéco, created in 1824 and still in use today.

➕ E6 ✉ place du Béguinage ☎ 217 8742 🕐 Tue, Sat 10–5; Wed–Fri 9–5 🚌 58, 61; tram 92, 93, 94 ♿ Good 🎟 Free

Above: Abbaye de la Cambre. Below: Notre Dame de la Chapelle, detail

BRUSSELS

See Top 25 Sights for
LA BASILIQUE DE KOEKELBERG (▶ 24)
CATHÉDRALE ST-MICHEL ET STE-GUDULE (▶ 36)
ÉGLISE NOTRE DAME DU SABLON (▶ 30)
ÉGLISE ST-JACQUES-SUR-COUDENBERG (▶ 34)

ABBAYE DE LA CAMBRE

Founded in 1201 for the Cistercian Order, the abbey was extensively rebuilt during the 16th and 18th centuries and now houses the National Geographical Institution. A 14th-century church is attached and there are elegant French gardens.

➕ G10 ✉ avenue E Duray ☎ 648 1121 🕐 Mon–Fri 9–12, 3–6; Sat 3–6; Sun 8–12:30, 3–6; Catholic feast days 9–12 🚌 Tram 23, 90, 94 ♿ Few 🎟 Free

COLLÉGIALE DES STS-PIERRE ET GUIDON

The Romanesque crypt is 11th century, but the superb Gothic church with frescos is from the 14th to 16th centuries. The long altar is illuminated by light filtering through the lovely stained glass above. The rare Celtic tombstone is believed to mark the grave of St Guidon.

➕ B8 ✉ place de la Vaillance ☎ 521 7438 🕐 Mon–Fri 9–12, 2–5:30. Closed during services 🚇 St Guidon/St Guido ♿ Few 🎟 Free

ÉGLISE NOTRE-DAME DE LA CHAPELLE

Pieter Bruegel the Elder was buried here, close to the rue Haute, where he was born. A memorial was erected by his son.

E8 ⊠ 4 rue des Ursulines ☎ 513 5348 ⏰ Summer: Mon–Sat 9–5; Sun 1–3.30. Winter: Mon–Sat 1–4; Sun 1–3.30 🚇 Gare Centrale/Centraal Station 🚌 20, 48 ♿ Few 🎫 Free

ÉGLISE NOTRE-DAME DE LAEKEN

This massive neo-Gothic church was commissioned by Leopold I and designed by Joseph Poelaert in 1851. It is the burial place of the Belgian royal family.

E3 ⊠ parvis Notre Dame ☎ 479 2362 ⏰ Guided tours Sun 2–5; services 1st Fri of month 5, Sat 5, Sun 9:15, 10:15, 11:30 🚌 53; tram 81 ♿ Few 🎫 Free

ÉGLISE STE-CATHERINE

Ste Catherine's, built by Poelaert in 1854 over part of the old port, is more attractive inside than out. A tower of the former 17th-century church survives.

E7 ⊠ place Ste-Catherine ☎ 479 8068 ⏰ Summer: Mon–Sat 8–6. Winter: Mon–Sat 8:30–5; Sun 8–12. Closed hols 🚇 Ste Catherine/St Katelijine ♿ Few 🎫 Free

ÉGLISE ST-NICOLAS

Brussels' oldest church, almost lost in the heart of the tourist area, was founded in the 11th century, but most of the interior dates from the 18th. The building is curved, as it once followed the line of the River Senne, and a cannonball in the wall recalls the city's bombardment of 1695.

E7 ⊠ 1 rue au Beurre ☎ 513 8022 ⏰ Mon–Sat 7:45–6; Sun 9–8 🚇 Bourse/Beurs 🚌 29, 34, 47, 48, 60, 63, 65, 66, 71, 95, 96; tram 23, 52, 55, 56, 81 (; ♿ Good 🎫 Free

BRUGES

See Top 25 Sights for
HEILIG BLOEDBASILIEK (► 48)
KATHEDRAAL ST- SALVATOR (► 40)
ONZE-LIEVE-VROUWEKERK (► 43)

JERUZALEMKERK

This 15th-century building was inspired by the basilica of the Holy Sepulchre in Jerusalem. Half of the original 12 almshouses attached to the church have survived and are now the Kantcentrum (lace centre ► 70).

dIII ⊠ Peperstraat 3a ☎ 33 00 72 ⏰ Mon–Fri 10–12, 2–6; Sat 10–1, 2–5. Closed hols 🚌 4, 6 ♿ Good 🎫 Inexpensive

SINT-WALBURGAKERK

Jesuit Pieter Huyssens built this splendid baroque church between 1619 and 1642, and the 17th-century oak pulpit is astonishing.

dIII ⊠ Sint-Maartensplein ☎ 34 32 57 ⏰ Summer: 8–10PM and occasionally during the day. Winter: only during Sunday services, 10, 7 🚌 6 ♿ None 🎫 Free

St-Jakobskerk

This beautiful church was founded c1420 in a neighbourhood of rich Brugean families and foreign delegations all made generous donations for the decoration of the building. The church has an extremely rich collection of paintings by Pieter Pourbus, Lancelot Blondeel and several anonymous Flemish Primitives.

bIII ⊠ Moerstratt ☎ 33 18 34 ⏰ July–Aug: daily 2–5:30. Sep–Jun: one hour before mass on Sat from 3; Sun from 11

Jeruzalemkerk

ARCHITECTURE

Bruegel and Erasmus

The 16th-century painter Pieter Bruegel was born in the Marolles (► 26) and his house at 132 rue Haute has been restored. The 16th-century humanist philosopher Erasmus spent five months in 1521 at 31 rue de Chapitre. This now contains an important collection of documents by him and his contemporaries as well as Renaissance furniture.

➕ F7 ☎ 521 1383 🕐 Wed, Thu, Sat–Mon 10–12 🚊 St Guidon/St Guido

Art nouveau Old England

BOURSE

The Belgian Stock Exchange is in an elegant 1873 building with a decorative frieze by Albert-Ernest Carrier-Belleuse and sculptures by Auguste Rodin.

➕ E7 ✉ 2 rue H Maus ☎ 509 1211 🕐 Mon–Fri only for groups by prior arrangement 🚊 Bourse/Beurs 🚋 Tram 23, 52, 55, 56, 81 ♿ Few ✋ Free

COLONNE DU CONGRÈS

This column designed by architect Joseph Poelaert, surmounted by a statue of Leopold I, was erected in 1850 to commemorate the National Congress of 1831. At the foot burns the flame honouring the Unknown Soldiers of both world wars.

➕ F7 ✉ place du Congrès 🚊 Madou ♿ Good ✋ Free

GALERIES ST-HUBERT

A covered arcade with new and old-fashioned shops, built in 1846–7, when this type of elegant shopping mall was a first in Europe.

➕ E7 ✉ rue du Marché-aux-Herbes 🚊 Gare Centrale/Centraal Station ♿ Good ✋ Free

LA MONNAIE

The original 1697 theatre, properly known as Théâtre Royal de la Monnaie was enlarged in 1819 by Napoleon to become one of the most beautiful in the world. It was here the Belgian Revolution began in August 1830. In 1985 the theatre was again enlarged, with a ceiling by Sam Francis and tiling by Sol Lewitt.

➕ E7 ✉ 4 rue Léopold ☎ 229 1211 box office (► 80) 🕐 Tours Sat at noon in French and Flemish only (30 minutes) 🚊 De Brouckère ♿ Very good ✋ Tour moderate

PALAIS DE JUSTICE

One of Leopold II's pet projects, designed by Poelaert in grand eclectic style. The interior is as overwhelming as the views over Brussels from the terrace. The Palais de Justice still contains the main law courts.

➕ E8 ✉ place Poelaert ☎ 508 6578 🕐 Mon–Fri 9–3. Closed hols 🚇 Louise/Louiza 🚋 Tram 92, 93, 94 ♿ Very good 🎟 Free

RÉSIDENCE PALACE

This luxurious art-deco apartment building was Brussels' largest; it is now offices. The sumptuous pool was inspired by the ruins of Pompeii.

➕ G7 ✉ 155 rue de la Loi ☎ 231 0305 🕐 Open only for events 🚇 Schuman

SERRES ROYALES (ROYAL GREENHOUSES)

Alophonse Balat and the young Victor Horta built this magnificient city of glass for Leopold II in the Brussels suburb of Laeken.

➕ F2 ✉ 61 avenue du Parc Royal (Domaine Royal, Laeken) ☎ 513 8940 (tourist information) 🕐 Only 2 weeks a year: end Apr–May when flowers are in bloom 🚇 Heysel/Heizel 🚋 53; tram 52, 92 ♿ Few 🎟 Free during the day, moderate at night (details from toursit office)

BRUGES

See Top 25 Sights for
BEGIJNHOF (▶ 41)
MARKT (▶ 46)
BURG (▶ 47)
GRUUTHUSE MUSEUM (▶ 44)
ST-JANSHOSPITAAL (▶ 42)

SINT-JANSHUYSMOLEN

The only one of the four windmills in Bruges that can be visited, the St-Janshuysmolen was built by a group of bakers in 1770 and was acquired by the city of Bruges in 1914. It still grinds grain. Inside is a small museum.

➕ dI ✉ Kruisvest ☎ 44 87 11 🕐 May–Sep: 9:30–12:30, 1:15–5 🚋 4, 6,16 ♿ None 🎟 Inexpensive

Seven Wonders

The *Septem admirationes civitatis Brugensis* (Bruges' Seven Wonders) by P. Claessins the Elder (1499–1576), in the *Beguinage*, depicts the Onze-Lieve-Vrouwekerk tower, the Halles and Belfry, as well as the House with the Seven Turrets. The Water Hall on the Markt, the Water House and Hansa House no longer exist; only the tower of the Poorters' Lodge remains.

Bruges' Belfry

ATTRACTIONS FOR CHILDREN

Brussels for children

Apart from parks and adventure parks, most activities for children happen indoors. Musée de Cinéma (► 82), Centre Belge de la Bande Dessinée (► 37), the musées d'Art Ancien et Moderne (► 32–3) and the Musée Royal de l'Afrique Centrale (► 51) have workshops for children of various ages. For details see *The Bulletin* (► 22).

Gaston Lagaffe/Guust Flater

BRUSSELS

See Top 25 Sights for
AUTOWORLD (► 38)
CENTRE BELGE DE LA BANDE DESSINÉE (► 37)
MUSÉE ROYAL D'ART ET D'HISTOIRE (► 38)
MUSÉE ROYAL DE L'ARMÉE ET D'HISTOIRE MILITAIRE (► 38)

BRUPARCK

Bruparck is like a miniature Europe with 350 models of monuments in the European Community and a launchpad for the Ariane space rocket.
🔳 D2 ⊠ 20 boulevard du Centenaire, Heysel ☎ 478 0550
🕐 Varies with season and attraction; phone first 🚇 Heysel/Heizel
🚻 Good 🎫 Very expensive

SCIENTASTIC MUSEUM

This fun museum gives kids the chance to experience science through exciting light, sound, smell and touch installations and exhibits.
🔳 E7 ⊠ Metro station Bourse/Beurs, 1st floor ☎ 736 5335
🕐 Jul, Aug: daily 2–5:30. Mid-Jan to Jul Sat,Sun 2–5:30. Closed mid-Dec to mid-Jan 🚇 Bourse/Beurs 🚻 Good 🎫 Moderate

WALIBI

Theme park with good rides, gentle carousels and a play area for children.
🔳 Off map ⊠ Freeway E411 Brussels-Namur, exit 6, in Wavres/Waveren ☎ 41 44 66 🕐 May–Aug: daily 10–6. Sep: Sat–Sun 10–6
🚆 Train from Gare Schuman to Gare de Bierges on Ottignies/Louvain-la-Neuve line (300m walk from station) 🚻 Few 🎫 Very expensive

BRUGES

BOUDEWIJNPARK

The 30 excellent attractions and shows here include an ice show and Europe's most sophisticated dolphinarium.
🔳 Off map ⊠ avenue De Baeckestraat 12, St. Michiels ☎ 38 38 38
🕐 May–Aug: daily 10–6. Apr & Sep: daily 11–6. Dolphinarium Mar–Oct: more than one ice show a day; Nov–Feb: show Sat, Sun and hols 4 🚊 7, 17 from the railway station 🚻 Good 🎫 Very expensive

DE ZEVEN TORENTJES (CHILDREN'S FARM)

This former 14th-century feudal estate with an authentic pigeon-house and gothic barn is now a children's farm with a fine playground.
🔳 Off map ⊠ Canadaring 41, Assebroek ☎ 35 40 43
🕐 Mon–Fri 8:30–noon, 2–4 🚊 2

PARKS

BRUSSELS

See Top 25 Sights for
PARC DE BRUXELLES (▶ 34)
PARC DU CINQUANTENAIRE (▶ 38)

BOIS DE LA CAMBRE

Once part of the Forest of Soignes, the Bois was annexed by the city in 1862 and laid out by landscape artist Keilig. Boating, fishing and roller-skating.

🔆 G11–G12 ☒ Main entrance on avenue Louise
🕐 Dawn–dusk 🚋 Tram 93, 94 🦽 Few 🖐 Free

FORÊT DE SOIGNES

A wonderful beech forest that includes Tervuren Arboretum ☎ 769 2081, Groenendaal Arboretum ☎ 657 0386 and Jean Massart Experimental Garden ☎ 673 8406.

🔆 G13–H13–J13–K 13 ☒ Boitsfort ☎ 629 3411/660 6417 🕐 Guided tours Thu and Sun at 10:30
🍴 Restaurant 🚋 Tram 44 🦽 None 🖐 Free

PARC DE LAEKEN

Enough to amuse you all day. Beyond its attractive lawns lie the Royal Residence and the amazing Royal Greenhouses (▶ 55).

🔆 E2 ☒ Main entrance on boulevard de Smet de Naeyer, Laeken
🕐 Dawn–dusk 🚇 Heysel/Heizel 🦽 Few 🖐 Free

PARC JOSAPHAT

With sculpture museum, animal reserve and sporting facilities. Free concerts Sundays in July and August.

🔆 G5–H5 ☒ Entrance on avenue des Azalées 🕐 Dawn–dusk
🍴 Café 🚋 Tram 23 🦽 Few 🖐 Free

BRUGES

See Top 25 Sights for
DE VESTEN EN POORTEN (RAMPARTS) (▶ 39)

KONINGIN ASTRIDPARK

Laid out in 18th-century English-country style, with a good children's playground.

🔆 cIII ☒ Main entrance Park 🕐 24 hours 🚌 1, 11 🦽 Good
🖐 Free

MINNEWATERPARK

On the edge of Lake Minnewater, with a sculpture garden and free concerts in summer.

🔆 bIV ☒ Arsenaalstraat 🕐 Dawn–dusk 🍴 Café-restaurant
🚌 All buses to the train station 🦽 Good 🖐 Free

Parc de Bruxelles

Brussels green spaces

Parks cover nearly 14 per cent of Brussels and provide an extremely high ratio of green space per inhabitant (27.5sq m). The parks in the centre, although well laid out, often feel charmingly unkempt and abandoned, particularly on weekends, when most people head for the woods and other green spaces just outside the city.

MARKETS IN BRUSSELS

Markets in Bruges

The weekly market on the Zand attracts large crowds every Saturday morning. Goods for sale range from clothes to household products, music and farm-made goat's cheese. On the nearby Beursplein, stands sell fruit, vegetables and flowers. A smaller food and flower market is held on the Markt (► 46) on Wednesday mornings. On Saturday and Sunday mornings from March to October there is an antiques and second-hand market on the Dijver and Vismarkt.

GARE DU MIDI

The Marché du Midi is one of Europe's largest and more exotic markets, with fresh fruit and vegetables, fish, meat, clothes, household goods, North African music, pictures and books.

✚ D8 ⊠ Near the Gare du Midi ⏰ Sun 7–1 🚇 Gare du Midi/Zuidstation 🚊 Tram 23, 52, 55, 56, 81, 82, 90 ♿ Few 🖐 Free

GRAND' PLACE

Small flower and plant market in the Grand' Place. On Sunday mornings there is a little more noise, as all kinds of bird – from canaries and parakeets to ducks, hens and doves – are sold in the bird market.

✚ E7 ⊠ Grand' Place ⏰ Flower market Tue–Sun 8–6. Bird market Sun 7–2 🚇 Bourse/Beurs 🚊 Tram 23, 52, 55, 56, 81 ♿ Good 🖐 Free

PLACE DE LA DUCHESSE DE BRABANT

The Brabant Province around Brussels is renowned for its strong horses, still used as draught horses on many Belgian farms. These beautiful animals, as well as racehorses, are sold here after much bargaining.

✚ C7–D7 ⊠ place de la Duchesse de Brabant ⏰ Fri 6–noon 🚇 Gare de l'Ouest/Weststation 🚊 63, 89 ♿ Few 🖐 Free

PLACE DU GRAND SABLON

The place du Grand Sablon is crowded with antique shops, but on weekends there is a small street market full of collectibles. Don't expect bargains!

✚ E8 ⊠ place du Grand Sablon ⏰ Sat 9–6; Sun 9–2 🚊 48; tram 91, 92, 93, 94 ♿ Few 🖐 Free

PLACE DU JEU DE BALLE

Sunday is definitely the best day to browse around this great junk market in the Les Marolles district. Arrive early for bargains.

✚ E8 ⊠ place du Jeu de Balle ⏰ Daily 7–2 🚊 48 ♿ Good 🖐 Free

Sunday bird market in the Grand' Place

CANALS IN BRUGES

Bruges is often referred to as 'the Venice of the North' and its *reien* (as the Flemish call their canals) provide much of its romantic charm although they are no longer used for public transport. Taking a boat on the canals is one of the best ways to explore the centre. Except when the canals are frozen, there are daily guided tours in several languages, including English. Illuminated evening tours offered in summer, are especially pleasant.

Canal along the Dijver

AUGUSTIJNENREI
One of the less spectacular canals, but nonetheless beautiful with the Augustijnen Bridge (*c*1425), and the adjacent Spaanse Loskaai road, whose name recalls Spanish presence in the 14th and 15th centuries.
✚ bll ▣ 3

DIJVER
The lovely little walkway along this canal shows off some of Bruges' grandest architecture: at No. 11 is the College of Europe, at No. 12 is the Groeninge Museum (➤ 45), and at No. 17 is the Gruuthuse Museum (➤ 44). In the summer there is a Saturday and Sunday junk market.
✚ blll ▣ 1, 6, 11, 16

GROENEREI/STEENHOUWERSDIJK
The view of this canal from the Vismarkt (Fish Market) is one of the most idyllic (and often-painted) in Bruges. The Meebrug and the Peerdenbrug are two of Bruges' oldest stone bridges. At the end of the Groenerei is the almshouse De Pelikaan (1634), which is well worth a visit.
✚ clll ▣ 1, 6, 11, 16

ROZENHOEDKAAI
Another wonderful corner, with rear views of the buildings of the Burg and the Huidenvettersplein, and of the famous Duc de Bourgogne Hotel.
✚ blll ▣ 1, 6, 11, 16

Minnewater
Lying to the south of Walplein and Wijngaarrdplein is the Minnewater or Lake of Love, which was the outer harbour of Bruges before the river silted up, cutting the city off from the sea. Named after a woman called Minna who, according to legend, fell in love with a man her father did not approve of. Desolate Minna hid in the woods around the lake, where she died before her lover could rescue her. Her lover parted the waters and buried her beneath the lake (➤ 55).

FESTIVALS & PROCESSIONS

BRUSSELS

MEIBOOM (RAISING OF THE MAYPOLE)

On 9 August a procession from the Sablon (➤ 30) to the Grand' Place (➤ 28) recalls an attack on a wedding party in 1213 by bandits from Leuven. The gang was foiled and the grateful duke allowed the party to plant a *meiboom*, or maypole, on their saint's feast day.

OMMEGANG

On the first Tuesday and Thursday in July, this colourful procession (literally 'doing the rounds') goes from the place du Grand Sablon (➤ 30) to the Grand' Place (➤ 28). Dating back to the 14th century, it celebrates the arrival of a statue of the Virgin from Antwerp. Nowadays it ends in a dance on the illuminated Grand' Place from 9PM to midnight. Dance tickets available from late May, are expensive and must be reserved in advance with the Brussels Tourist Office ✉ Town Hall, Grand' Place, 1000 Brussels ☎ 513 8940, fax 514 4538

Ommegang *procession*

Carnivals

Several Belgian cities, including Brussels and Bruges, celebrate Carnival around mid-February, with a procession and the election of the Carnival Prince. The main event is on Shrove Tuesday, Mardi Gras, when people dressed in richly embroidered costumes and masks dance in the cities' main squares to ward off evil spirits (information from the tourist offices ➤ 90).

BRUGES

GOUDEN BOOMSTOET (PAGEANT OF THE GOLDEN TREE)

This magnificent procession, held in August 2000 and every five years thereafter, re-enacts the festivities for the wedding of Charles the Bold and Margaret of York, celebrated in Bruges.

HEILIG BLOEDKAPEL PROCESSION

Every year at 3PM on Ascension Day (May) the relic of the Holy Blood (➤ 48) is taken out in a spectacular procession involving thousands of participants. Scenes in the procession tell stories from the Bible, as well as the legend of the coming of the Holy Blood to Bruges and the worship of the relic. Information from Bruges Tourist Office ✉ Burg 11, ☎ 44 86 86

BRUSSELS & BRUGES
where to...

BELGIUM'S BEST DINING

Prices

Expect to pay the following per person for a three-course meal without drinks:

£££   over 1,500Bf

££   750–1,500Bf

£   under 750Bf

The king of Belgian food

Chef Pierre Wynants, owner and chef of the famous Comme chez Soi restaurant, listed on this page, is an authority on Belgian and European food. He has transformed Belgium's cuisine and has put traditional ingredients like Belgian beer and hop shoots on his menus.

BRUSSELS

L'ALBAN CHAMBON (£££)

Brilliant French food here served perfectly in plush surroundings. Specialities include potatoes with shrimp and truffles, and scallops with truffle vinaigrette.

⊞ E7 ⊠ 31 place de Brouckère ☎ 217 7650 ⏰ Mon–Fri lunch, dinner. Closed hols 🚇 De Brouckère 🚃 Tram 23, 52, 55, 56, 81, 90

LA BELLE MARAÎCHÈRE (££–£££)

Well-known traditional fish restaurant on Brussels' old harbour. The delicious *waterzooi* (fish stew) with three fishes is excellent and the set menus are great value.

⊞ E7 ⊠ 11 place Ste-Catherine ☎ 512 9759 ⏰ Fri–Tue lunch, dinner 🚇 Ste Catherine/St Katelijne or Bourse/Beurs 🚃 Tram 23, 52, 55, 56, 81, 90

BRUNEAU (£££)

Traditional Belgian food at its very best in a sumptuous setting. Specialities include ravioli with celery and truffles, and the superb crusty duck breast is simply divine.

⊞ C5 ⊠ 73–5 avenue Broustin ☎ 427 6978 ⏰ Thu–Mon lunch, dinner 🚇 Basilique

COMME CHEZ SOI (£££)

By common consent Belgium's finest restaurant (quite something in a country with so many fine restaurants), with

---

specialities such as sweetbreads with hop shoots and sole fillets with Riesling mousseline and shrimps. Reserve some weeks ahead.

⊞ E7 ⊠ 23 place Rouppe ☎ 512 2921 ⏰ Tue–Sat lunch, dinner. Closed Dec 24–Jan 1 🚇 Anneessens 🚃 Tram 23, 52, 55, 56, 81

L'ECAILLER DU PALAIS ROYALE (£££)

The perfect place to take a Belgian minister or banker. The decor is stuffy and bourgeois, the clientele serious and respectable and the food always impeccable, with excellent *croquettes aux crevettes* (shrimp croquettes) and Zeeland oysters and a wonderful grilled turbot on tomato coulis. Reserve a week ahead.

⊞ E8 ⊠ 18 rue Bodenbroeck ☎ 512 8751 ⏰ Mon–Sat lunch, dinner 🚃 34, 95, 96; tram 92, 93, 94

LA MAISON DU CYGNE (£££)

Dine on truffles, rich mousses, and *foie gras* in this luxurious restaurant with great views of the Grand' Place. Go with an empty stomach and a full wallet.

⊞ E7 ⊠ 9 Grand' Place ☎ 511 8244 ⏰ Mon–Fri lunch, dinner; Sat dinner only 🚇 Gare Centrale/Centraal Station

LA MANUFACTURE (££)

This pleasant modern restaurant in the old Delvaux leather factory serves delicious and inventive European food with a touch of Asia quite rare in Brussels. Courtyard tables in summer.

✚ D7 ✉ 12 rue Notre-Dame du Sommeil ☎ 502 2525 🕓 Mon–Fri lunch, dinner; Sat dinner 🚇 Bourse/Beurs 🚋 Tram 23, 52, 55, 56, 81, 90

LES QUATRE SAISONS (££–£££)

Widespread praise confirms the reason for this restaurant's popularity. Try the poached sole with crayfish crème and mushrooms, or the salad of lobster and smoked goose liver with balsamic cream.

✚ E7 ✉ 5 rue de l'Homme Chrétien ☎ 505 5100 🕓 Sun–Fri lunch, dinner; Sat dinner. Closed mid Jul–mid Aug 🚇 Bourse/Beurs 🚋 Tram 23, 52, 55, 56, 81, 90

BRUGES

AMBROSIUS (££)

This cosy rustic serves wonderful French and Belgian cuisine. There is a terrace in the summer and a log fire in winter.

✚ biv ✉ Arsenaalstraat 53–5 ☎ 34 41 57 🕓 Wed–Sun dinner 🚌 1, 2, 11

DEN GOUDEN HARYNCK (££–£££)

The fine chef in this typically Brugean restaurant prepares the freshest ingredients without too many frills. Specialities include pleasant surprises like smoked lobster with fig chutney and scallops with goose liver.

✚ blll ✉ Groeninge 25 ☎ 33 76 37 🕓 Tues–Sat lunch, dinner 🚌 1

DE KARMELIET (£££)

Often regarded as Bruges' best restaurant, De Karmeliet serves the inspired Belgian cuisine of Geert Van Hecke in a stylish high-ceilinged mansion.

✚ clll ✉ Langestraat 19 ☎ 33 82 59 🕓 Mon–Sat lunch, dinner; Sun lunch

'T PANDREITJE (£££)

The fish is excellent in this much-lauded restaurant, particularly the smoked eel pie. There are several *dégustation* menus as well as à la carte dishes, and the setting is comfortably plush, with service in the lovely garden in summer.

✚ clll ✉ Pandreitje 6 ☎ 33 11 90 🕓 Mon, Tue, Thu–Sat lunch, dinner 🚌 1, 6, 11, 16

DE SNIPPE (£££)

At this popular restaurant in a well-restored 18th-century house, master chef Luc Huysentruyt – disciple of Auguste Escoffier the late chef and author – displays his flair for innovation and his strong roots in tradition. His amazing fish dishes are his speciality.

✚ clll ✉ Nieuwe Gentweg 53 ☎ 33 70 70 🕓 Tue–Sat lunch, dinner; Mon dinner 🚌 1, 11

Bruges anno 1468

Celebrate on 3 July, 1468, the anniversary of Charles the Bold and Margaretha of York with a gigantic four-course dinner. Beer and wine flow, and minstrels, knights, dancers and fire eaters entertain. Reservations esssential.

✉ Vlamingstraat 86, 8000 Bruges ☎ 34 75 72 🕓 Apr–Oct: Fri evening, Sat. Rest of the year: Sat only

BRASSERIES & FRITERIES

Frites, frites, frites...

Belgium claims the best chips in the world. The secret of their *frites* is that they are fried twice and thrown in the air to get rid of the extra oil. Every Belgian has a favourite *friterie* or *frietkot*, but most agree that Homage à Mafrite on the place du Jeu de Balle in Brussels is one of the best.

BRUSSELS

L'ACHEPOT (£–££)

Popular, casual place where real Brussels cuisine is served. Offal dishes are the speciality – sweetbreads, brains, veal kidneys and liver.
✉ 1 place Ste-Catherine
☎ 511 6221 ⏰ Mon–Sat lunch, dinner 🚇 St. Catherine/St Katelijne or Bourse/Beurs

AU STEKERLAPATTE (£)

This dark maze of a restaurant serves a long menu of traditional Belgian dishes – among them *poularde de Bruxelles au champignons* (chicken with mushrooms) and excellent steak tartare. With its friendly service and a good atmosphere, it draws other restaurateurs on their day off.
➕ E8 ✉ 4 rue des Prêtres
☎ 512 8681 ⏰ Tue–Sun dinner 🚇 Hôtel des Monnaies/Munthof

CHEZ LEON (££)

In the most famous of all Belgian mussels restaurants, large portions of shellfish are well prepared in many different ways.
➕ E7 ✉ 18 rue des Bouchers
☎ 513 0426 ⏰ Daily noon–11 🚇 Bourse/Beurs

IN 'T SPINNEKOPKE (££)

This rustic restaurant serves Belgian dishes such as *waterzooi* and rabbit cooked in *gueuze* beer. Cosy atmosphere with welcoming log fires.
➕ E7 ✉ 1 place Jardin aux

Fleurs ☎ 511 8695
⏰ Sun–Fri lunch, dinner; Sat dinner 🚇 Ste Catherine/St Katelijine or Bourse/Beurs

LE PAIN QUOTIDIEN (£)

In this chain of tearooms, breakfast, lunch, snacks and afternoon tea are served around one big table. The big, old-fashioned breads, croissants, pastries and jams are all homemade.
➕ E8 ✉ 11 rue des Sablons
☎ 513 5154 ⏰ Mon–Sat 7:30–7; Sun 8–7 🚇 4, 95; tram 20, 48
➕ E7 ✉ 16 Rue Antoine Dansaert ☎ 502 2361

TAVERNE DU PASSAGE (£–££)

This elegant brasserie founded in 1928, certainly does not show its age. It is charming, renowned for its *croquettes au crevettes* (shrimp croquettes) and ultra-traditional Brussels cuisine. The *choucroute au jambon* (saurerkraut with ham) is a must.
➕ E7 ✉ 30 Galerie de la Reine ☎ 512 3731 ⏰ Daily noon–midnight 🚇 Gare Centrale/Centraal Station

DE ULTIEME HALLUCINATIE (££)

This is worth a visit just for the splendid art-nouveau interior, but the French food also lives up to expectation. The goose- and duck-liver specialities and poached fish in *gueuze* sauce are truly delicious. Popular café.
➕ F6 ✉ 316 rue Royale
☎ 217 0614 ⏰ Mon–Fri 11–2; Sat 5PM–3AM
🚇 Botanique/Kruidtuin

VINCENT (££)

Off the busy rue des Bouchers and not very touristy, this beautifully tiled brasserie serves traditional Brussels cuisine like mussels and *carbonnades* (charcoal-grilled meats). Because you walk through the steaming kitchen to reach your table, with ingredients hanging from the window, you see what you are going to eat.

➕ E7 ✉ 8–10 rue des Dominicains ☎ 502 3693 🕐 Daily lunch, dinner 🚇 Bourse/Beurs

---

BRUGES

CAFEDRAAL (££)

Hidden seafood restaurant where you'll find *waterzooi* and an excellent North Sea bouillabaisse. Beautiful torchlit garden terrace.

➕ blll ✉ Zilverstraat 38 ☎ 34 08 45 🕐 Tue–Sat lunch, dinner 🚌 1, 2, 3, 4, 5, 8, 9, 11, 13, 16

CHEZ OLIVIER (££)

This cosy place is in an old house with fine views over one of the prettiest canals, and the French fare is simple but stylish.

➕ clll ✉ Meestraat 9 ☎ 33 36 59 🕐 Mon–Fri lunch, dinner; Sat dinner. Jun–Aug: closed lunch 🚌 6, 16

BREYDEL DE CONINCK (£)

Popular mussel restaurant regarded as the best by many locals, despite its uninspired setting.

➕ blll ✉ Breidelstraat 24 ☎ 33 97 46 🕐 Thu–Tue

lunch, dinner. Closed Jun 🚌 1, 3, 4, 6, 8, 11, 13, 16

DEN DIJVER (££)

All dishes here, both meat and fish, are lovingly prepared with Belgian beer. The interior is old Flemish, and the view from the terrace summer is great.

➕ blll ✉ Dijver 5 ☎ 33 60 69 🕐 Summer: Thur–Tue. Winter: Thur–Mon. Lunch, dinner 🚌 1, 6, 11, 16

KINDERS CISKA (£–££)

This Knokke institution, founded in 1842, serves the best waffles in town. There are several Ciska outlets but this one has a great playground.

➕ Off map ✉ Oosthoekplein 1, Knokke-Heist ☎ 60 20 08 🕐 Jul–Aug: daily lunch, dinner . Apr, May, Jun, Sep, Oct: Wed–Mon lunch. Nov–Mar: lunch, dinner weekends only

LE PAIN QUOTIDIEN (£)

Excllent snacks throughout the day.

➕ blll ✉ Philip Stockstraat 21 ☎ 33 60 50/33 67 66 🚌 All buses

SIPHON (££)

This hugely popular restaurant outside Bruges serves Flemish specialities such as river eel in green herb sauce and grilled T-bone steaks. Very good value for money. Reserve well ahead.

➕ Off map ✉ Damse Vaart Oost 1 ☎ 62 02 02 🕐 Sat–Wed lunch, dinner 🚌 1.5km from Damme (➤ 21)

Belgian specialities

There is more to Belgian food than *moules frites*. *Waterzooi* is a little-known national dish, a delicate green stew of fish or chicken with leeks, parsley and cream. Plain but delicious, *stoemp* is potatoes mashed with vegetables, often served with sausages. *Carbonnade flamande* is beef braised in beer with carrots and thyme, and *lapin à la gueuze* is rabbit stewed in *gueuze* beer with prunes. *Anguilles au vert*, river eels in green sauce, is another popular dish.

INTERNATIONAL CUISINE

BRUSSELS

AU THÉ DE PEKIN (£)
Authentic Hong Kong cuisine and some Far Eastern fare are served in this simple room. Very good value.
🔢 E7 ✉ 16–24 rue de la Vierge Noire ☎ 513 4642 🕐 Daily lunch, dinner 🚇 Bourse/Beurs

LES BAGUETTES IMPERIALES (£££)
Belgium's best Asian restaurant, with refined Vietnamese dishes.
🔢 D2–D3 ✉ 70 avenue Jean Sobieski ☎ 479 6732 🕐 Mon, Wed–Sat lunch, dinner; Sun lunch 🚇 Stuyvenbergh 🚋 19, 23

BONSOIR CLARA (££)
This colourful, ultra-trendy restaurant serves light, modern Mediterranean food. Try the red tuna tartare or the ravioli stuffed with quail.
🔢 E7 ✉ 22–6 rue Antoine Dansaert ☎ 502 0990/5557 🕐 Mon–Fri lunch, dinner; Sun lunch 🚋 Tram 23, 52, 55, 56, 81

LA CANNE À SUCRE (££)
Caribbean cuisine and amazingly, more than 400 different rums.
🔢 E8 ✉ 12 rue de Pigeons, Sablon ☎ 513 0372 🕐 Tue–Sat dinner 🚋 20, 48; tram 91, 92, 93, 94

CASTELLO BANJI (££)
Excellent art-nouveau Italian restaurant. Try the delicious beef *carpaccio* with truffles in season and spinach lasagne.
🔢 E8 ✉ 12 rue Bodenbroek

☎ 512 8794 🕐 Tue–Sat lunch, dinner; Sun lunch 🚋 20, 48; tram 91, 92, 93, 94

CHEZ FATMA (£–££)
Fatma and Fergani Loussaifi, the king and queen of couscous, preside over the city's favourite Tunisian restaurants.
🔢 G8 ✉ 18 place Jourdan ☎ 230 9597 🕐 Mon–Fri lunch, dinner; Sat dinner 🚋 80

COMME CHEZ MOI (£)
Russian and Romanian cuisine in the heart of the Marolles district. Come for caviar and blini and a few shots of vodka or Russian wine.
🔢 E8 ✉ 140 rue Haute ☎ 502 5209 🕐 Tue–Sat lunch, dinner 🚋 20, 48

DA KAO (£)
Popular eatery serving good Vietnamese food to a trendy crowd ready for a long night.
🔢 E7 ✉ 38 rue Antoine Dansaert ☎ 512 6716 🕐 Daily lunch, dinner 🚇 Bourse/Beurs 🚋 Tram 23, 52, 55, 56, 81

KASBAH, RESTAURANT & SALON (££)
A delightful dark blue cave of a place, this popular Moroccan restaurant surprises with its large menu of *tajines* (stew cooked in an earthenware pot), couscous and grills accompanied by Arabic music. The Sunday brunch is excellent and very good value.
🔢 E7 ✉ 20 rue Antoine Dansaert ☎ 502 4026

Indonesian influences

Chinese food is rarely authentic in Belgian restaurants, which often get more inspiration from Indonesian cuisine. Almost every menu offers *loempia*, a big spring roll, or *nasi goreng*, Indonesian fried rice. And don't worry about the spices: as most dishes are adapted to suit Belgian tastes you are unlikely to be putting your tastebuds at risk.

🕐 Sun–Fri lunch, dinner; Sat
dinner 🚇 Bourse/Beurs
🚊 Tram 23, 52, 55, 56, 81

NEOS COSMOS (££)

Lively Greek café serving
excellent mezze in an
attractive, contemporary
setting.
➕ E7 ✉ 50 rue Antoine
Dansaert ☎ 511 8058
🕐 Daily lunch, dinner
🚇 Bourse/Beurs 🚊 Tram 23,
52, 55, 56, 81

LES PERLES DE PLUIE (££)

A wonderful Thai
restaurant in a beautiful
Brussels house.
➕ F9 ✉ 56 rue de Châtelein
☎ 649 6723 🕐 Tue–Sun
lunch, dinner; Sat dinner
🚊 Tram 93, 94

BRUGES

BHAVANI (£–££)

Bruges' best Indian
restaurant specialises in
tandoori and vegetarian
dishes.
➕ blll ✉ Simon Stevinplein 5
☎ 33 90 25 🕐 Wed–Mon
lunch, dinner 🚌 All buses

BODEGA LORENA (££)

Senor Rodrigues, the
master of *tapas*, serves
more than 60 here along
with plenty of good wines
and good beer.
➕ blll ✉ Loppemstraat 13
☎ 34 88 17 🕐 Tue–Sat
dinner 🚌 All buses

DE LANGE MUUR (££–£)

This Chinese restaurant
serves specialities from
Canton, Fukien, and
Peking and is renowned
for its Chinese fondue and

rijsttafels (spicy dishes
with plain rice).
➕ blll ✉ St-Amandsplein 11
☎ 33 27 19 🕐 🕐 Daily
lunch, dinner 🚌 All buses

MANGE TWO (££)

French gastronomy is
fused with influences from
around the world,
prepared by the former
chef of the liner *QE 2*.
➕ clll ✉ Langestraat 16
☎ 49 02 25 🕐 Fri–Tue lunch,
dinner; Thu dinner only
🚌 6, 16

TANUKI (££)

Classic Japanese dishes in
an authentic setting with
plenty of wood, a rock-
tiled floor and a bamboo
garden. Excellent sushi
and tempura.
➕ blV ✉ Oude Gentweg 1
☎ 34 75 12 🕐 Wed–Fri
lunch, dinner 🚌 1, 11

TRIUM (£)

Bruges' best Italian
restaurant serves fresh
pasta and crunchy pizzas,
and the waiters are some
of the most charming
outside Italy.
➕ blll ✉ Academiestraat 23
☎ 33 30 60 🕐 Tue–Sun
lunch, dinner 🚌 4

Bad news for vegetarians

If you don't eat meat you may
find it difficult to eat in Belgium,
as most of the country's
traditional dishes include meat
amd Belgian restaurants provide
only a salad or an omlette with
chips as vegetarian dishes. In
some fish dishes are an option,
including the famous 'moules-
frites'. Heading for an oriental
restaurant is another, particularly
Thai or Indian.

BARS & CAFÉS

A glass of beer

There are more than 400 varieties of Belgian beer. *Lambic* is a beer that ferments spontaneously; the yeast for fermentation is not added by the brewer but is that found naturally in the local air. *Gueuze* is a mixture of *lambics*, while sweet *kriek* is *lambic* with cherries. Trappist beers come as *doubels* with 6–7 per cent alcohol or *tripels* at 8 or 9 per cent. Refreshing and lighter is *bierre blanche* or *witbier*, made of wheat and often drunk with a slice of lemon. Many of these beers come with their own glasses, specially designed to make the most of the beer's flavour and perfume. In the café La Lunette on the place de la Monnaie, every 'lunette' comes in a one-litre coupe (like an outsized champagne glass). In winter Belgians like to have a tiny glass of *jenever*, a popular local spirit similar to gin – guaranteed to warm you up!

BRUSSELS

A LA MORT SUBITE
This traditional bar was once among singer Jacques Brel's favourite watering holes and is still popular. It even has its own brew, called 'Morte Subite' (Sudden Death) because of its higher alcohol content.
E7 ✉ 7 rue Montagne aux Herbes Potagères ☎ 513 1318 🕐 Mon–Sat 11AM–1AM, Sun 12:30PM–1AM 🚇 Gare Centrale/Centraal station

L'ACROBATE
Kitsch bar full of plastic roses, madonnas and bright colours. Frequent live concerts and dancing in the back after midnight.
E7 ✉ 14 rue Borgval ☎ 513 7308 🕐 Fri, Sat 9–dawn 🚇 Bourse/Beurs 🚊 Tram 23, 52, 55, 56, 81, 90

AU SOLEIL
Popular bar in a former old-fashioned men's clothing shop. Tables outside in summer.
E7 ✉ 86 rue du Marché au Charbon ☎ 513 3430 🕐 Daily 10AM–2AM 🚇 Bourse/Beurs 🚊 Tram 23, 52, 55, 56, 81, 90

L'ESPÉRANCE
Panelled art-deco bar with a discreet staircase to upstairs rooms. Once popular with politicians and now just a funky place for drinks.
E6 ✉ 1–3 rue du Finistère ☎ 217 3247 🕐 Mon–Fri 10AM–1AM 🚇 De Brouckère

LE FALSTAFF
At some time during an evening out everyone usually ends up at this huge but always busy art-deco café with a vast terrace that's heated in the winter.
E7 ✉ 19–25 rue Henri Maus ☎ 511 9877 🕐 Mon–Fri 10.30AM–3AM; Sat, Sun 10:30AM–5AM 🚇 Bourse/Beurs 🚊 Tram 23, 52, 55, 56, 81, 90

KAFKA
Smoky dark bar with a wide selection of vodkas and Belgian beers, local eccentrics and dusty habitués. Pleasant and slightly bookish, the place mellows later at night when the vodka loosens up the rather serious Flemish intellectuals among its patrons.
E7 ✉ 6 rue de la Vierge Noire ☎ 513 5489 🕐 Daily 4PM–3AM 🚇 De Brouckère

LE JAVA
Small, noisy bar – the perfect place to end a night on the town.
E7 ✉ 14 rue St-Géry ☎ 512 3716 🕐 Mon–Sat 8PM–3AM; Sun noon–3AM 🚇 Bourse/Beurs 🚊 Tram 23, 52, 55, 56, 81, 90

LE SUD
Good music and unreal Arabesque-Eurotrash decor. The Clo-Clo club in the cellar is a must if you long to hear 1970s French *chanson* (song). Worth searching out.
E7 ✉ 43 rue de l'Ecuyer (no sign, big sun mask above the entrance) 🕐 Tue–Sun after 10PM 🚇 De Brouckère

DE ULTIEME HALLUCINATIE
(▶ 64–65)

ZEBRA

Simple red-brick walls, outdoor terrace and good music, Zebra is in a lively and popular nightlife area. Open from breakfast onwards.

🏠 E7 ☒ 35 place St- Géry ☎ 511 0901 🕔 Daily 7:30AM–1AM or later Ⓢ Bourse/Beurs 🚋 Tram 23, 52, 55, 56, 81

BRUGES

BISTRO DU PHARE

Popular hang-out for locals serving a large variety of Belgian beers and fresh snacks. There is a pleasant garden terrace in summer.

🏠 cII ☒ Sasplein 2 ☎ 34 35 90 🕔 10AM–midnight or later 🚌 4

CHAGALL

This cosy bar-restaurant serves Belgian specialities such as eel, rib steaks and mussels to the accompaniment of classical music. Good choice for a coffee during the day or for an after-dinner liqueur.

🏠 bIII ☒ Sint-Amandstraat 40 ☎ 33 61 12 🕔 Daily lunch, dinner 🚌 All buses

DA GARRE

Located down a tiny alley between the Burg and Markt, this 16th-century bar has a huge selection of Belgian beers. Plays classical music.

🏠 bIII ☒ De Garre 1 ☎ 34 10 29 🕔 Mon–Thu noon–mignight; Fri–Sun noon–1AM 🚌 All buses

DE LOKKEDIZE

This popular candle-lit jazz café is often full, although the noisiest tipplers stay around the bar. Light snacks.

🏠 bIII ☒ Korte Vulderstraat 33 ☎ 33 44 50 🕔 Tue–Thu 7PM–3AM; Fri–Sun 6PM–3AM or later 🚌 4, 8

'T BRUGS BEERTJE

The place for true beer lovers, with 300 traditionally brewed Belgian beers – many of them rare and for sale only here and all served in their special glass. The atmosphere is as Belgian as can be, and the landlord is always happy to help you choose a beer.

🏠 bIII ☒ Kemelstraat 5 ☎ 33 96 16 🕔 Thu–Tue 4PM–1AM 🚌 All buses

'T EI

Trendy bar-restaurant where good simple *tapas* are served to the latest music. DJ on Saturday nights; occasional live music.

🏠 bIII ☒ Eiermarkt 13 ☎ 33 20 85 🕔 Tue–Sun 2–10PM, bar open later during weekends 🚌 All buses

DE VLISSINGHE

Reputedly the oldest café in Bruges, built around 1515, this is popular with locals as well as visitors. Relaxed and easy-going.

🏠 cIII ☒ Blekerstraat 2 ☎ 34 37 37 🕔 Wed–Mon 11AM–until the customers go home 🚌 4, 8

Beer in Bruges

There are two breweries in the town centre. De Gouden Boom (☒ Verbrand Nieuwland ☎ 33 2697) makes Tarwebier, a wheat beer that's good with a slice of lemon, and a stronger brew called Brugse Tripel with a 9.5 per cent alcohol content. De Straffe Hendrik (☒ Walplein 26 ☎ 33 26 97) brews another wheat beer with a sweet aroma.

LACE

Fabrics and lace

In the 13th century, Belgium was already famous for woven fabrics and intricate tapestries, made from English wool and exported as far as Asia. By the 16th century, Brussels was renowned for the fine quality of its lace. Lace remains one of the most popular traditional souvenirs of Brussels and Bruges but few Belgian women learn the craft today. As a result, there is not enough handmade lace to meet the demand, and what there is has become very expensive. Many shops now sell lace made in China, which costs less but is inferior.

BRUSSELS

LACE GALLERY

Tiny old-fashioned shop specialising in good-quality handmade lace blouses, tablecloths, umbrellas, cushion covers.
➕ E7 ✉ 30 rue du Lombard, corner rue de l'Etuve ☎ 513 5830 ⏰ Daily 10–7
🚇 Bourse/Beurs 🚊 Tram 23, 52, 55, 56, 81, 90

LACE PALACE

Everything that can possibly be made of lace, both Belgian and imported, old and new. Spacious.
➕ E7 ✉ 1–3 rue de la Violette ☎ 512 5634 ⏰ Daily 8:30–8 🚇 Gare Centrale/Centraal Station

RUBBRECHT

Exquisite old lace pieces, tablecloths and blouses, as well as new Belgian handmade lace. Definitely a cut above the rest.
➕ E7 ✉ 23 Grand' Place ☎ 512 0218 ⏰ Mon–Sat 9:30–7; Sun 10–6 🚇 Gare Centrale/Centraal Station

TOEBAC

One of the better lace shops on a street lined with them. Wide selection of blouses, tablecloths, and modern and antique lace, mostly Belgian-made.
➕ E7 ✉ 10 rue Charles Buls ☎ 512 0941 ⏰ 9:30–7
🚊 Tram 23, 52, 55, 56, 81, 90

BRUGES

'T APOSTELIENTJE

This small pretty shop offers professional advice about lacemaking, as well as the tools to make lace, together with ready made old and modern lace available to buy.
➕ dIII ✉ Balstraat 11 ☎ 33 78 60 ⏰ Mon–Sat 9:30–6; Sun 11–4 🚊 6, 16

GRUUTHUSE LACE SHOP

The place to look for fine lace, especially antique pieces. All lace is made in Belgium. Handmade porcelain dolls dressed in antique lace are another speciality.
➕ bIII ✉ Dijver 15 ☎ 34 30 54 ⏰ Summer: daily 10–7. Winter: daily 10–6:30 🚊 1, 6, 11, 16

KANTCENTRUM (LACE CENTRE)

Historical and technical exhibits. Afternoon lacemaking demonstrations, and lacemaking materials on sale. Interesting courses.
➕ dIII ✉ Peperstraat 3a ☎ 33 00 72 ⏰ Mon–Fri 10–12, 2–6; Sat 10–1, 2–5. 🏷 Inexpensive

KANTJUWEELTJE (LACE JEWEL)

Wide selection of handmade new and antique Flemish lace and tapestries. Lacemaking demonstrations take place at 3 PM daily.
➕ bIII ✉ Philipstockstraat 11 ☎ 33 42 25 ⏰ Summer: daily 9–7. Winter: daily 9–6 🚊 4, 8

CRAFTS, SOUVENIRS & GIFTS

BRUSSELS

AU GRAND RASOIR (MAISON JAMART)

A beautiful specialist knife shop, supplier to the royal family, with an incredible selection for every possible purpose. Repairs, sharpening, re-silvering.

✚ E7 ✉ 7 rue de l'Hôpital (place St-Jean) ☎ 512 4962 🕐 Mon–Sat 9:30–6:30 🚊 Gare Centrale/Centraal Station 🚌 34, 48, 95, 96

THE BRUSSELS CORNER

The souvenirs here are of a better quality and more fun than elsewhere with a large collection of T-shirts and gift boxes filled with Belgian beers.

✚ E7 ✉ 27 rue de l'Etuve ☎ 511 9849 🕐 Daily 9:30–6:30 🚌 34, 48

LA BOUTIQUE DE TINTIN

Tintin fans come here for everything from pyjamas, socks, cups and diaries to life-size statues of Tintin and his friend Abdullah and, of course, the books in several languages.

✚ E7 ✉ 13 rue de la Colline ☎ 514 5152 🕐 Tue–Thu 10–6; Mon 2–6 🚊 Gare Centrale/Centraal Station

CHRISTA RENIERS

Beautiful contemporary jewellery with a touch of Zen and no shortage of humour. Reniers' silver cufflinks and keyrings are fun, and the bracelets, rings and earrings have an elegance all their own.

✚ E7 ✉ 29 rue Antoine Dansaert ☎ 514 1773

🕐 Mon–Sat 10:30–6:30 🚌 23; tram 23, 52, 55, 56, 63, 81

KASOERI

A great fabric shop – look for linen in natural colours, silks, wools, brightly colored Indian cottons and buttons made of coral and mother-of-pearl.

✚ F8 ✉ 20 rue de la Paix ☎ 514 2251 🕐 Mon–Sat 10:30–6:30 🚊 Porte de Namur/Naamse Poort

BRUGES

BRUGS DIAMANTHUIS

The technique of diamond polishing is attributed to the mid-15th century Bruges goldsmith van Berquem and Bruges was Europe's first diamond city. This shop keeps alive the tradition of diamond polishing and offers a large selection of quality diamonds and diamond jewellery.

✚ cIII ✉ Cordoeaniersstraat 5 ☎ 34 41 60 🕐 Mon–Fri 10–12, 1:30–5; Sat 10–3 🚌 6, 16

KERAMIEK ANNE PERNEEL

Unusual, earthy ceramics for everyday use and ornate flowerpots for the garden. It is wonderful to see this inventive potter at work and somehow her enthusiasm is contagious.

✚ cIII ✉ Genthof 29 ☎ 82 38 38 🕐 Sat 10–12, 1:30–6 🚌 4, 8

Original birthday presents

At *Dans la presse ce-jour-là* (in the press that day) you'll find original copies of newspapers in several languages – buy one printed on the recipient's day of birth (✉ 126 rue Antoine Dansaert ☎ 511 4389). Or how about a life-size Manneken Pis fountain for the garden? Just look in the shops around Manneken Pis (➤ 27) on the rue de l'Etuve.

BOOKS

Expensive business

The Belgian mark up on foreign books is often high, so it is a good idea to bring your reading matter from home or shop in second-hand shops. In addition, the Deslegte chain sells second-hand books and discounted new books (✉ 17 rue des Grandes Carmes, Brussels ☎ 511 6140 ✉ Vlamingstraat 37–9, Bruges ☎ 34 04 39).

BRUSSELS

BRÜSEL
Large bookshop selling famous comic strips such as Tintin and Asterix, mainly in French but also in English, Dutch, German and Spanish.
✚ E7 ✉ 100 boulevard Anspach ☎ 502 3552 🕐 Mon–Sat 10:30–6:30 🚋 Tram 23, 52, 55, 56, 81

FNAC
Brussels' largest bookshop, with books in French and Dutch as well as a good selection of English, German, Italian and Spanish books and a good music department.
✚ F6 ✉ City 2, rue Neuve ☎ 209 2211 🕐 Mon–Thu, Sat 10–7; Fri 10–8 🚇 Rogier or De Brouckère 🚋 Tram 23, 52, 55, 56, 81

P GENICOT
Books from the 17th century to the present day, mainly French but some in English. Lovely.
✚ E7 ✉ 6 galerie Bortier on 19 rue St-Jean ☎ 514 1017 🕐 Mon–Sat noon–7 🚇 Gare Centrale/Centraal Station

IMAGE
Books in several languages on Belgian monuments, architecture and monument conservation packed into a small shop.
✚ E7 ✉ 72 rue de la Montagne ☎ 512 2272 🕐 Mon–Fri 11–5 🚇 Gare Centrale/Centraal Station

WATERSTONES
Part of the British chain, with a good selection of English language books and magazines.

✚ E6 ✉ 71–5 boulevard Adolphe Max ☎ 219 2708 🕐 Mon, Wed–Sat 9–6:30; Tue 10–6:30 🚇 Rogier 🚋 Tram 23, 52, 55, 56, 81

TROPISMES
Very open and stylish bookshop in an elegant gallery with a wide selection of books on art, architecture, history and philosophy, plus English-language books. Good coffee-table books and French literature are a speciality. Pleasant for browsing.
✚ E7 ✉ galerie des Princes ☎ 512 8852 🕐 Mon, Sun 1:30–6:30; Tue–Thu, Sat 10–6:30; Fri 10:30–8 🚇 Gare Centrale/Centraal Station

BRUGES

DE REYGHERE
Books in Flemish, French, English and German and a wide selection of international newspapers and magazines.
✚ blll ✉ Markt 12 ☎ 33 34 03 🕐 Mon–Thu, Sat 8:30–6:15; Fri 8:30–7 🚌 All buses

RAAKLIJN
Bruges' best bookshop has a good selection of foreign-language books, especially paperbacks and art books.
✚ blll ✉ St-Jacobsstraat 7 ☎ 33 67 20 🕐 Mon–Sat 9–6:30 🚌 All buses

ANTIQUES & SECOND-HAND

BRUSSELS

ANTIK BLAES
Two floors of funky, old European furniture, old shop furniture and a few intriguing curiosities.
✚ E8 ✉ 51–3 rue Blaes ☎ 512 1299 ⏰ Daily 10–6 🚌 20, 21, 48

GALERIE MODERNE
This huge auction house handles everything from top-of-the-market antiques to junk and bric-à-brac.
✚ F8–G8 ✉ 3 rue du Parnasse ☎ 511 5415 ⏰ Twice a month. Phone for viewing times 🚇 Trône/Troon 🚌 38, 54, 60, 95, 96

GALERIE VANDERKINDERE
This expensive auction house specialises in art and objects from the 17th and 18th centuries.
✚ D11–E11 ✉ 512 rue Leon Vanderkindere ☎ 344 5446 ⏰ Mon–Fri 9–12, 2–5. Phone for times of sale 🚌 38; tram 23, 55, 38

GHADIMI
Oriental carpets, kilims and textiles – mainly 19th-century – are stylishly presented in this bright, cheerful gallery.
✚ E8 ✉ 1 rue des Minimes, just off the place du Grand Sablon ☎ 512 9841 ⏰ Tue–Sun 10–12, 2–6 🚌 34, 48, 95, 96; tram 92, 93, 94

HISTORIC MARINE
Old and antique boat and ship models as well as antique compasses, marine instruments and paintings of boats. Other selected nautical paraphernalia.

✚ E7 ✉ 39a rue du Lombard ☎ 513 8155 ⏰ Mon–Sat 9:30–5:30 🚌 34, 49, 95, 96

PUCCI
A fascinating shop full of art-deco and art-nouveau chandeliers, furniture and objects d'art.
✚ E8 ✉ 13 rue de la Paille ☎ 512 7889 ⏰ Mon–Sat 10–5:30 🚌 34, 48, 95, 96

STYLE & KEZOEN
A wide selection of old fountain pens from famous manufacturers are bought, sold and repaired in this shop.
✚ E8 ✉ 124 rue Blaes ☎ 387 0122 ⏰ Tue, Thu–Sat 9–2 🚌 20, 48

BRUGES

THEATER GALERY VAN MULLEM
Small shop hidden on this pretty square with antique Flemish furniture, unusual lights and wonderful paintings.
✚ bIII ✉ Vlamingstraat 52 ☎ 33 41 41 ⏰ Mon–Thu, Sat 10–12, 2–6 🚌 All buses

ROYAL STEWART ANTIQUES
Silver and 18th- and 19th-century furniture, as well as 19th-century paintings.
✚ dIII ✉ Genthof 25 ☎ 33 79 18 ⏰ Mon–Thu, Sat 10–7; Fri 2–5 🚌 4, 8

Antiques in Brussels
Go to Brussels' Sablon area (➤ 30) for fine antiques, and to the junk market in the Marolles (➤ 26, 58) if you want to browse or bargain hunt. *Brocante* – old collectibles – and antique shops on rue Haute and the rue Blaes are good for furniture but becoming fashionable, so the prices aren't the bargains they once were. Check out the streets behind the church on place du Jeu de Balles.

FOOD

Belgian biscuits

Pain à lo Grecque is a light crispy biscuit covered in tiny bits of sugar, while *speculoos* is a finer version of gingerbread. The *coucque de Dinant* is a hard, bread-like biscuit that comes beautiful shapes – windmills, rabbits, peasants, cars and more.

BRUSSELS

AU SUISSE
The traditional deli to buy smoked fish, cheeses, *charcuterie* (cold cuts) and other delicacies. Try the house speciality, *filet Américain*, a steak tartare. The sandwich bar next door of the same name is also a Brussels institution.
➕ E7 ✉ 73–5 boulevard Anspach ☎ 512 9589
🕐 Mon–Sat 8:30–7
🚇 Bourse/Beurs 🚋 Tram 23, 52, 55, 56, 81

BIÈRE ARTISANALE
Over 400 Belgian beers and their appropriate glasses. The gift packages make good presents.
➕ F8 ✉ 174 Chausée de Wavre ☎ 512 1788
🕐 Mon–Sat 11–7 🚇 Porte de Namur/Naamse Poort

DANDOY
A beautiful bakery, founded in 1829, selling traditional Brussels biscuits such as *pain à la Grecque*, *speculoos* and *coucque de Dinant* in all sizes and shapes, as well as Belgium's best marzipan. Once you are inside, this place is hard to resist!
➕ E7 ✉ 31 rue au Beurre (new branch 14 rue Charles Buls) ☎ 511 0326 🕐 Mon–Sat 8:30–6:30; Sun 10–6:30 🚇 Bourse/Beurs 🚋 Tram 23, 52, 55, 56, 81

LE PAIN QUOTIDIEN
(► 64)

WITTAMER
This wonderful but seriously expensive patisserie sells the best sorbets in town, excellent handmade chocolates and cakes that taste as good as they look.
➕ E8 ✉ 12–13 place du Grand Sablon ☎ 512 3742
🕐 Mon 8–6; Tue–Sat 7–7; Sun 7–6 🚋 34, 48, 95, 96; tram 92, 93, 94;

BRUGES

DELDYCKE
Wide selection of Belgian and other cheeses, *charcuterie* and prepared salads, as well as wine and liqueurs.
➕ bIII ✉ Wollestraat 23 ☎ 33 43 35 🕐 Wed–Mon 9–2, 3–6:30 🚌 1, 6, 11, 16

TEMMERMAN
Good old-fashioned sweets, sugared almonds, *speculoos* and fine handmade chocolates in the shape of sea creatures or pebbles, all stored in large jars. Try the heart-shaped *peperkoek*, a spicy honey bread, or the interesting fruity teas.
➕ bIII ✉ Zilverpand, Noordzandstraat 63 ☎ 33 16 78 🕐 Mon 2–6:30; Tue–Thu 10–12:30, 2–6:30; Fri, Sat 10–6:30 🚌 All buses

WOOLSTREET COMPANY
A small shop selling more than 450 Belgian beers and their special glasses.
➕ bIII ✉ Wollestraat 31a ☎ 34 83 83 🕐 Daily 10–7 🚌 1, 6, 11, 16

BELGIAN CHOCOLATES

BRUSSELS

GALLER

Very good pralines and delicious chocolate bars in many flavours. Belgian Royal Warrant Holder.

✚ E7 ✉ 44 rue au Beurre
☎ 502 0266 🕐 Daily 10–9:30 🚇 Bourse/Beurs
🚊 Tram 23, 52, 55, 56, 81

GODIVA

The most famous chocolatier of all, with shops around the world.

✚ E7 ✉ 22 Grand' Place
☎ 511 2537 🕐 Mon–Sat 9AM–midnight; Sun 10AM–midnight 🚇 Gare Centrale/Centraal Station

MARY'S

This old-fashioned chocolate shop, specialising in fine home-made pralines and wonderful marrons glacés, is well known among Brussels' chocolate lovers. Specialities include truffles and florentines and traditional handmade chocolates.

✚ F6–F7 ✉ 73 rue Royale
☎ 217 4500 🕐 Tue–Fri, Sat 2–5 🚇 Botanique/Kruidtuin
🚊 Tram 92, 93, 94

NEUHAUS

The most beautiful of the many Neuhaus branches, with divine Belgian chocolates in astonishing gift boxes. Try specialities like Caprice (chocolate with nougatine and fresh cream) or Temptation (with coffee and fresh cream).

✚ E7 ✉ 25–7 Galerie de la Reine ☎ 512 6359
🕐 Mon–Sat 9–8; Sun 10–7 🚇 Gare Centrale/Centraal

Station 🚇 Bourse/Beurs
🚊 Tram 23, 52, 55, 56, 81

PLANÈTE CHOCOLAT

'Chocolate is art' is Frank Duval's slogan. You can watch him make and sculpt wonderful artworks or pralines on the premises from the best chocolate. If you're a serious chocoholic don't miss the first floor tearoom, with its selection of chocolates, cakes and ice creams.

✚ E7 ✉ 24 rue du Lombard
☎ 511 0755 🕐 Daily 9–6:30, on fine, summer days until 10pm 🚇 Bourse/Beurs 🚊 Tram 23, 52, 55, 56, 81

WITTAMER (▶ 74)

BRUGES

DEPLA

Delicious handmade chocolates. Specialities include truffles, florentines, chocolates with nuts and raisins and good marzipan wrapped in chocolate. There is another branch at Eekhoutstraat 23.

✚ blll ✉ Huidenvettersplein 13 ☎ 34 74 12 🚊 6, 16
🕐 Daily 10–6:30

GODIVA

The Bruges branch of this chocolatier.

✚ blll ✉ Zuidzandstraat 36
☎ 33 28 66 🕐 Mon–Sat 9–12:30, 2–7 🚊 All buses

SWEERTVAEGHER

Superior and luxurious handmade pralines, much appreciated by Brugeans.

✚ blll ✉ Philipstockstraat 29
☎ 33 83 67 🕐 Tue–Sat 9:30–6:30 🚊 6, 16

Chocolate chains

The Swiss claim that they produce the best chocolate in the world is hotly disputed in Belgium. The Swiss may market it more effectively, but Belgian chocolate is as good if not better. The Leonidas chain, less expensive than the shops mentioned here, sells very good quality chocolates and the beautifully wrapped Côte d'Or bars are worth seeking out in supermarkets.

BELGIAN FASHION

Brussels shopping streets

Avenue Louise (➤ 35) is the traditional shopping area, with everything from Chanel to the Belgian designer Olivier Strelli. The fashionable place to shop, however, is rue Antoine Dansaert, which has the best shoe shops in Brussels and several shops of new designers. Most Belgian designers, including Walter Van Bierendonk, Ann Demeulemeester, Dries Van Noten, Dirk Bikkembeug, Veronique Branquiinho and Chris Mestdagh (the Belgian Paul Smith), have flagship shops in Antwerp, but are available at the Stijl, the large specialty shop that is the grand temple of Belgian fashion. All these designers produce an accessible avant-garde fashion, while designers such as Chine and Olivier Strelli produce more commercial clothes, while Kaat Tilley stands out for her amazingly textured clothes. Apart from the several Stijl shops, other shops and new designers have opened their doors on Dansaert including Annemie Verbeke.

BRUSSELS

CHINE
This Belgian designer brings in Hong Kong designs of very wearable fashion, mainly silk, wool and cotton dyed in beautiful colours.
➕ E7 ✉ 2 rue Van Antevelde ☎ 503 1449 🕓 Mon–Sat 10–6:30 🚇 Bourse/Beurs 🚋 Tram 23, 52, 55, 56, 81

ELVIS POMPILLO
This Liège-born hatmaker – who really *is* called Elvis Pompillo – makes some very wearable and some outrageous hats for men, women, and kids – always with a quirky twist.
➕ E7 ✉ 10 rue du Midi ☎ 511 1188 🕓 Mon–Sat 10:30–6:30 🚋 34, 38; tram 23, 52, 55, 56, 8134, 48

KAAT TILLEY
Tilley's loose, sculptured clothes for women in luscious fabrics defy description, while the shop belongs in a fairy tale. Her clothes are hugely popular in Japan and in New York, where she has now opened two more shops.
➕ E7 ✉ 4 Galerie du Roi ☎ 514 0763 🕓 Mon–Fri 10–6; Sat 10:30–6:30 🚇 Gare Centrale/Centraal Station 🚋 29, 63, 66, 71

OLIVIER STRELLI
Streamlined, modern fashion for men and women primarily in blacks, beiges, greys and browns, with only an occasional dash of colour.
➕ F9 ✉ 72 avenue Louise ☎ 512 5607 🕓 Mon–Sat 10–6 🚋 Tram 93, 94

STIJL
This fashion giant sells the collections of established designers such as Dries Van Noten, Bikkembergs, as well as the newcomers, in bare and cold industrial surroundings. You'll find men's and women's clothes here and sister shops down the street selling trendy children's clothes (Kat en Muis) and beautiful lingerie (Stijl Underwear, 47 rue Antoine Dansaert).
➕ E7 ✉ 74 rue Antoine Dansaert ☎ 512 0313 🕓 Mon–Sat 10:30–6:30 🚋 63; tram 23, 52, 55, 56, 81

BRUGES

L'HEROÏNE
The only shop in Bruges with a wide selection of Belgian fashion designers, including Kaat Tilley, Chris Janssens and Dries Van Noten. Also fashion accessories and Belgian jewellery.
➕ blll ✉ Zilverpand 5, Noordzandstraat 57b ☎ 33 56 57 🕓 Mon–Sat 10–6:30 🚌 All buses

OLIVIER STRELLI
A branch of the Brussels' fashion store.
➕ blll ✉ Eiermarkt 3 ☎ 34 38 37 🕓 Mon–Sat 10–6 🚌 All buses

OFFBEAT & UNUSUAL

BRUSSELS

AZZATO

Musical instruments, especially string instruments and flutes. Also ethnic instruments, particularly drums.

✚ E7 ✉ 42 rue de la Violette
☎ 512 37 52 🕐 Mon–Sat
9:30–6 🚊 Bourse/Beurs
🚋 Tram 23, 52, 55, 56, 81

IDIZ BOGAM

Very good and fashionable selection of second-hand clothes and shoes. A branch is at 76 rue Antoine Dansaert.

✚ E8 ☎ 162 rue Blaes
☎ 502 8337 🕐 Daily
10:30–6 🚋 20, 48 🚊 Porte
de Hal/Hallepoort

PICARD

Europe's largest party store is a wonderful place. Fancy dresses for sale or rent, masks, party tricks and magicians' equipment.

✚ E7 ✉ 71–5 rue du
Lombard ☎ 513 0790
🕐 Mon–Sat 9–6 🚋 34, 48

ROYAL DOG SHOP

'Le Couturier pour Chiens' says it all. Diamond collars, cardigans, raincoats and accessories for Fido, made to measure or ready-made.

✚ E7 ✉ 27–28 place de la
Justice/Justitieplein ☎ 513
3261 🕐 Mon, Wed–Sat 9–6
🚋 34, 48

SERNEELS

A spacious shop with a wonderful selection of toys from tiny ducklings to full-size camels and cars, as well as old-fashioned rocking horses.

✚ F9 ✉ 69 avenue Louise
☎ 538 3066 🕐 Mon–Sat
9:30–6:30 🚋 Tram 93, 94

THEO DEPOT OPTIEK

The funkiest optician in town with glasses 'to be seen in' – nothing is too extravagant.

✚ E7 ✉ 81 rue Antoine
Dansaert ☎ 511 0447
🕐 Mon–Sat 10.30–6 🚋 63;
tram 23, 52, 55, 56, 81

BRUGES

DE WITTE PELIKAAN

In this shop you can feel in a Christmas mood all year round with Christmas wrappings and tree decorations from around the world.

✚ bIII ✉ Vlamingstraat 23
☎ 34 82 84 🕐 Mon–Sat 11–6
🚋 All buses

OUD TEGELHUIS

Amusing shop in two old houses stocking all kinds of bygone tins and posters.

✚ cIII ✉ Peerdenstraat 11
☎ 34 01 03 🕐 Tue–Sun 10–6
🚋 1, 6, 11, 16

ROMBAUX

Lovely old-fashioned shop with CDs, instruments and sheet music.

✚ cIII ✉ Mallebergstraat 13
☎ 33 25 75 🕐 Mon–Sat
9–12:30, 2–6:30 🚋 All buses
to the Markt

Old-fashioned toys

The De Krokodil chain sells beautifully made wooden toys, mobiles, puppets and creative toys and musical instruments. Pricey but worth every franc.

✉ 47 rue des Fripiers, Brusssels
☎ 217 4397

✉ St-Jacobsstraat 47, Bruges
☎ 32 75 79

JAZZ, POP & NIGHTLIFE

Nightspots

From elegant art-nouveau cafés and smoky old joints full of local pensioners to the crowded bars of rue du Marché au Charbon, you'll find it all within walking distance of the Grand' Place. As there are so many good bars to meet their friends Belgians socialise a great deal. Most Brussels clubs open at 11PM but don't start to fill before midnight – don't start out too early. The English and Australians, used to drinking up before the pubs close at 11PM, may need some stamina. It is customary to buy rounds for your friends or whoever paid the last one.

BRUSSELS

L'ACROBATE (► 68)

ANCIENNE BELGIQUE

One of Brussels' best rock venues, revamped as ashowcase for the Flemish community and a counterpart to the Botanique (see below), mounts regular concerts by major artists. A smaller club on the first floor hosts other gigs.

✚ E7 ✉ 114 boulevard Anspach ☎ 584 2400 🚊 Tram 23, 52, 55, 56, 81

BEURSSCHOUWBURG

The 19th-century theatre of the Stock Exchange is now a venue for rock concerts, good jazz, North African rai and avant-garde Belgian theatre.

✚ E7 ✉ 22 rue Auguste Orts ☎ 548 2424 🚊 34, 47, 48, 63, 95, 96; tram 23, 52, 55, 56, 81

BOTANIQUE

The splendid botanical gardens were turned into a cultural centre for Brussels' French-speaking community. There are regular rock concerts in the Orangerie and, increasingly, world music events such as the Festival de la Chanson (Festival of Song), held indoors and out during September.

✚ F6 ✉ 236 rue Royale ☎ 226 1211 🚇 Botanique 🚊 38, 61; tram 92, 94

CARNOA QUEBRADA

One of several Latin American clubs in this area. Strong, smooth *caipirinhas* cocktails make it easy to salsa.

✚ E7 ✉ 53 rue du Marché au Charbon ☎ 511 1354 🕐 Tue 9:30–early morning; Wed–Sun 10:30–dawn 🚊 Tram 23, 52, 55, 56, 81

CIRQUE ROYAL

Great circular hall in a former circus, with usherettes to show you to your seat. Good gigs.

✚ F7 ✉ 81 rue de l'Enseignement ☎ 218 2015 🚇 Madou 🚊 63

EXITO 13

South American club with good values on Latino food, fine jazz and the best Brazilian salsa groups.

✚ E8 ✉ 13 rue Haute ☎ 511 0038 🕐 Tue–Sat 7PM until the customers go home 🚊 20, 48

LE FOOL MOON

Trendy venue where concerts are followed by evenings in the same style. Dance-based acts, soul and acid-jazz. Excellent DJs.

✚ C7–D7 ✉ 126 quai de Mariemont ☎ 410 1003 🕐 Sat only 🚇 Gare l'Ouest/Weststation 🚊 63; tram 18

FOREST NATIONAL

One of Belgium's largest venues draws many major bands and stars despite the bad acoustics and endless parking problems.

✚ C11 ✉ 36 avenue du Globe ☎ 347 0355 🕐 All year round, times vary 🚊 48, 54; tram 18, 52

THE FUSE

Brussels' first techno club maintains excellent standards, with DJs from London, the States and

Amsterdam. The place is drab, but the crowds don't notice.

➕ E8 ✉ 208 rue Blaes
☎ 511 9789 🕐 Sat 11PM–7AM
Ⓜ Porte de Hal 🚍 20, 48

KK (KULTUURKAFEE)

Smoky student club at the Flemish University, with free weekly gigs by small local and European bands, good art films and interesting exhibitions.

➕ H–J10 ✉ VUB campus boulevard du Triomphe ☎ 629 3056 🕐 Concerts Oct–end Apr
🚍 43; tram 23, 90

MAGASIN 4

This former warehouse is where many up-and-coming rock bands perform for the first time in the country. It's a great place to watch new Flemish bands as well.

➕ E6 ✉ 4 rue du Magasin
☎ 223 3474 🕐 Check listings Ⓜ Yser/Isjer
🚍 Tram 18

MIRANO CONTINENTAL

Fashionable crowds of thirtysomethings frequent this former cinema where house music is king.

➕ G7 ✉ 38 chaussée de Louvain ☎ 218 5772 🕐 Sat 11PM–late Ⓜ Madou
🚍 29, 63

NEW YORK CAFÉ JAZZ CLUB

Smart, brasserie-type restaurant with jazz venue behind featuring local acts. Popular with celebrities.

➕ F8 ✉ place Stéphanie
☎ 534 8509 🕐 Thu–Sat 10PM–late Ⓜ Louise/Louiza
🚍 91, 92, 93, 94

LE SUD (► 68)

UPSIDE DOWN

Bar with paintings of tribesmen on the walls, a dance floor at the back, and DJs playing African music, soul and funk. Occasional live music.

➕ E7 ✉ 24 rue du Lombard
☎ 511 0093 🕐 Daily 7PM–4AM 🚍 34, 48, 95, 96; tram 23, 52, 55, 56, 81, 90

BRUGES

DE CACTUS CLUB

The main venue in town for rock, jazz and world music. The club also organises an open-air festival in Minnewater Park during the second weekend of July. A music café at No. 36 on the same street is hugely popular with locals.

➕ bIII ✉ St-Jacobsstraat 33
☎ 33 20 14 🚍 3, 13

DE VERSTEENDE NACHT

Cosy, smoky café run by a jazz aficionado. Often free jazz concerts weekends.

➕ cIII ✉ Langestraat 11
☎ 34 32 93 🕐 Tue–Thu 7PM–2AM; Fri 7PM–4AM

VILLA ROMANA

Popular mock Roman club especially crowded on weekends.

➕ bIII ✉ Kraanplein 1 ☎ 34 34 53 🕐 Daily 10PM–late
🚍 3, 4, 6, 8, 13, 16

Gay Brussels

The two lesbian bars are Le Feminin (✉ 9 rue Borgval 🕐 Tue, Thu–Sat 10PM–late) and Sapho (✉ 1 rue St-Géry 🕐 Fri, Sat 10PM–late). There are bars for gay men around rue des Pierres in addition to Le Belgica (✉ 32 rue du Marché au Charbon), Le Duquesnoy (✉ 12 rue Duquesnoy) with barmen in leather, and La Démence (✉ 208 rue Blaes).

Gay Bruges

The Bruges gay scene located on the outskirts of the city, is low key. Boomerang is the gay centre with Café del Mar for gays and lesbians (✉ Spoorwegstraart, St-Michiels). Ravel is also a gay bar (✉ Karel de Stoutelaan 172 ☎ 31 52 74).

OPERA & CLASSICAL MUSIC

Music by the coal stove

L'Atelier (✉ 51 rue du Commerce ☎ 511 2065 🚇 Trône/Troon), the former workshop of a painter and his wife who were both music lovers, is filled with canvases and memorabilia and is now a popular place for concerts. In the winter it is heated by a big coal stove in the middle of the room.

BRUSSELS

CHAPELLE ROYALE
Beautiful small hall with perfect acoustics, a favourite with chamber orchestras. Book early.
➕ F7–F8 ✉ 5 Coudenberg ☎ 673 0581 🚇 Gare Centrale/Centraal Station

CONSERVATOIRE ROYALE DE MUSIQUE
Another perfect venue for chamber orchestras, partly designed by the famous organ builder Cavaillé-Coll.
➕ F7 ✉ 30 rue de la Régence ☎ Box office 507 8200, in the Palais de Beaux Arts 🚇 Gare Centrale/Centraal Station

ÉGLISE DES ST-JEAN ET ST-ETIENNE AUX MINIMES
Many concerts are held in this high-baroque church near the Marolles quarter. The Philharmonic Society has early-music recitals, and on Sundays the La Chapelle des Minimes ensemble performs Bach cantatas. Admission fees are voluntary.
➕ E8 ✉ 62 rue des Minimes ☎ 511 9384 🕐 Lunchtime throughout the summer. One Sun a month at 10:30AM 🚌 48

PALAIS DES BEAUX ARTS
This art-nouveau complex is Brussels' most prestigious concert venue. Its two halls, which have perfect acoustics, are home to the Philharmonic Society and the Orchestre National de Belgique. This is where you will find most of the city's big concerts.
➕ F7 ✉ 23 rue Ravenstein ☎ Box office 507 8200, 24-hour information 507 8444 🕐 Box office Mon–Sat 11–6 🚇 Parc/Park or Gare Centrale/Centraal Station

THÉÂTRE DE LA MONNAIE
The national opera house is Brussels' pride. Since a sumptuous renovation in the 1980s, innovation and excellence have been hallmarks, first under Gerard Mortier and now under director Bernard Foccroulle, himself a musician. Performances sell out well in advance. (► 54).
➕ E7 ✉ place de la Monnaie ☎ 229 1211 🕐 Box office Tue–Sat 11–5:30 🚇 De Brouckère

BRUGES

Bruges hosts several classical music festivals a year, including the Flanders Festival, which takes place in churches all over the city in summer. For information check with the tourist office.

CULTUURCENTRUM
Good classical concerts.
➕ bIII ✉ St-Jacobsstraat 20–26 ☎ Info 44 30 40, box office 44 30 60 🕐 Box office Mon–Fri 10–1 and 2–6, Sat 10–1 🚇 All buses

THEATRE & DANCE

BRUSSELS

CIRQUE ROYAL (► 78)
The best dance theatre, mostly with contemporary dance.

KAAITHEATER
Influential, mainly Belgian, artists such as Anne Teresa de Keersmaeker, Jan Fabre and Maatschappij Discordia regularly perform here. More dance than theatre.

✚ E5–E6 ✉ 2 quai des Péniches ☎ Information 201 5858; box office 201 5959 🚇 Yser/Isjer

LUNATHEATER
A jewel of 1930s architecture, this former cinema houses the Flemish Theatre Institute. Occasional performances in English.

✚ D6 ✉ 20 place Sainctelettesquare ☎ Box office 201 5959 🚇 Yser/Isjer

THÉÂTRE 140
Rather scruffy but with excellent performances, both dance and theatre, by the best touring troupes.

✚ H6 ✉ 140 avenue Eugène Plasky ☎ 733 9708 🕐 Box office Mon–Sat 11–6 🚌 29, 63; tram 23, 90

THÉÂTRE NATIONAL
The National Theatre often arranges co-productions with Strasbourg. Most plays are in French, with the occasional English-speaking touring company.

✚ F6 ✉ Centre Rogier, place Rogier ☎ 203 5303 🕐 Box office Mon–Sat 11–6 🚇 Rogier

THÉÂTRE ROYAL DU PARC
Stunning theatre with excellent French productions as well as old-fashioned and now unique 1930s *pièces de boulevard* (experimental theatre that was originally performed in the street).

✚ F7 ✉ 3 rue de la Loi ☎ 512 2339 🕐 Box Office daily 11–6 🚇 Arts–Loi/Kunst–Wet or Parc/Park

THÉÂTRE DE TOONE
Adorable little marionette theatre, famous for productions of classics such as *Hamlet* and *Faust* performed in Bruxellois, the Brussels dialect, a strange mixture of French and Flemish. The café is fun and open all day.

✚ E7 ✉ 6 impasse Schuddeveld, petite rue des Bouchers ☎ 511 7137 🕐 Tue–Sat noon–midnight 🚇 Gare Centrale/Centraal Station

BRUGES

CULTUURCENTRUM
Four venues under one name, including the Stadsschouwburg, the city's theatre, with performances mostly in Flemish.

✚ bIII ✉ St-Jacobsstraat 20–26 ☎ 44 30 40, box office 44 30 60 🕐 Box office Mon–Fri 10–1, 2–6; Sat 10–1 🚌 All buses

Belgium dances

Belgium's reputation for contemporary dance has flourished since Frenchman Maurice Béjart founded his Twentieth Century Dance Company and the Mudra school in 1953 – and revolutionised dance in the country. There are now more than 50 companies in residence in Brussels, most of them very contemporary. The new choreographers Anne Teresa De Keersmaeker and Wim Vandekeybus are already famous around the world.

CINEMAS

Subtitles and dubbing

Foreign films in Bruges' cinemas are always subtitled; in Brussels you may find a dubbed version. If you care, be alert in the listings in daily newspapers or the English-language *Bulletin* for the following abbreviations: *VO* means *version originale*, subtitled; *V fr*, French version; *V angl*, English version; *EA* means *enfants admis*, children admitted; *ENA* means children under 16 are not admitted.

BRUSSELS

ACTORS STUDIO
Small two-screen repertory cinema presenting five films a day, mainly "B" films and good films from non-European countries.
✚ E7 ✉ 16 petite rue des Bouchers ☎ 0900 27 854 Ⓜ Gare Centrale/Centraal Station

ARENBERG GALERIES
This tiny but delightful cinema in a converted art-deco theatre in the Galeries St-Hubert specialises in repertory cinema films and foreign films. It's an excellent place to see some of the better films coming out of Asia and the Middle East.
✚ E7 ✉ 26 galerie de la Reine ☎ 0900 27 865 Ⓜ Gare Centrale/Centraal Station

KINEPOLIS
Vast film theatre complex in the Bruparck with 25 screens and the largest IMAX screen in Europe (it seats 7,000). Mainstream films, mainly Hollywood stuff.
✚ D2 ✉ Bruparck (➤ 56), 1 avenue du Cinquantenaire ☎ Bookings 474 2604, French information 0900 35 241, Flemish information 0900 35 240 Ⓜ Heysel/Heizel

MUSÉE DU CINÉMA
Besides the permanent exhibition, five films are shown daily, two of which are silent films accompanied by piano music. This is the place to see the old cinema classics, as well as more recent films and little-known jewels from Third World countries.
✚ F7 ✉ 9 rue Baron Horta ☎ 507 83 70 Ⓖ Daily 5:30–10:30 Ⓜ Gare Centrale/Centraal Station ▣ 20, 29, 38, 60, 63, 65, 66, 71, 95, 96; tram 92, 93, 94

UGC DE BROUCKÈRE
Ten well-equipped auditoriums, including the 70mm UCG Gran Eldorado. Mainly Hollywood productions.
✚ E7 ✉ 38 place De Brouckère ☎ 0900 10 440 (French), 0900 10 450 (Flemish) Ⓜ De Brouckère

BRUGES

KENNEDY
The two cinemas here screen most of the mainstream films as well as art films on certain evenings.
✚ bIII ✉ Zilverstraat 14 ☎ 33 20 70 Ⓖ See newspapers or display at the tourist office ▣ All buses

LUMIÈRE
The Theatre De Korre's two screens feature mainly foreign "B"films and better Belgian productions.
✚ bIII ✉ St-Jacobsstraat 36 ☎ 33 88 50 ▣ All buses

SPORTS

CYCLING

Not suprising in such a flat country, cycling is big in Belgium. Most races are in the countryside. The Grand Prix Eddy Merckx, named after one of the greatest Belgian cyclists, draws speed cyclists to Brussels in May–June. To cycle yourself, you can rent a bicycle from railway stations as well as from special agencies (➤ 90–91). The Forêt de Soignes (➤ 57) in Brussels has pleasant, very good cycle tracks and the ride from Bruges to Damme or to Knokke (➤ 21) has several splendid views.

FOOTBALL

All major cities have good football clubs, which can easily be reached by public transport. Bruges has two football teams in the Belgian first division, Club Brugge and Cercle Brugge. RSC Anderlecht, Belgium's most popular team, is often in European competitions and is an arch rival of Club Brugge. Belgium and Holland host the European Championships in the year 2000.

RSC Anderlecht ⊠ Vanden Stock stadium, 2 avenue Theo Verbeeck ☎ 522 1539 ⓠ St Guidon/St Guido ☎ Club Brugge 40 21 21 ☎ Cercle Brugge 38 91 93 ⊠ Olympialaan 🚊 25

GOLF

There are over 60 golf courses in Belgium; information can be obtained from the Fédération Royal Belge de Golf ☎ 067 22 04 40

JOGGING

In Brussels, most people jog in the Parc du Cinquantenaire (➤ 38), in the Parc de Bruxelles (➤ 34) or in the beautiful lanes of the Parc de Woluwe ⊠ avenue de Tervueren 🚊 Tram 39, 44 In Bruges, jog in the parks around the city (➤ 39) or in Tillegembos woods, St-Michiels ☎ 38 02 96 🚊 25 The Brussels 20km run, held annually on the last Sunday in May, attracts more than 20,000 competitors (Bruxelles Promotion 1886 ☎ 511 9000. The Ivo Van Damme Memorial, one of Brussels' most important athletic events, is in August. The Brussels Marathon is in September. Information from the tourist office. ☎ 513 8940

ROLLER SKATING

Patinoire Du Heysal (Brussels Roller Club) ⊠ 134 avenue de Madiudlaen ☎ 426 3804 ⓠ Heysel/Heizel Le Gymnase, an open-air rink ⊠ Bois de la Cambre Chemen du Gymnase ☎ 649 7002 ⓒ Summer only 🚊 Tram 23, 90, 93, 94

WALKING

The best place for a long walk near Brussels' centre is the Fôret de Soignes (➤ 57). Maps are available from the tourist office. In Bruges, you can walk in Tillegembos (see above) or along the canal to Damme (➤ 21).

Racing at the Hippodrome

Horse racing is becoming increasingly popular and there are several racetracks around Brussels. Events often feature chariot-style racing rather than races with the more conventional mounted jockeys.

Hippodrome de Boitsfort:

⊠ 51 chausée de la Hulpe

☎ 660 2839 🚊 41; tram 94

Hippodrome de Groenendael:

⊠ 54 St-Jansbergen, Hoeilaart

☎ 657 3820 🚊 366

Hippodrome de Sterrebeek

⊠ 43 avenue du Roy de Blicquylaan ☎ 767 5475

🚊 30; tram 39

HOTELS

Prices

Expect to pay the following for a double room with breakfast

£ less than 3,000Bf

££ 3,000–7,000Bf

£££ more than 7,000Bf

Cheap hotels

Many hotels in Brussels are business-orientated, so in summer and at weekends, prices can drop by up to 50 per cent. The Belgian Tourist Reservations office on Grand' Place (☎ 513 7484, fax 513 9277) has a free list of over 800 hotels offering off-peak reductions. Although this makes it difficult to reserve far in advance, hotels are rarely full in these periods. Bed-and-breakfast accommodation can be arrranged in Brussels (☎ 646 0737, fax 644 0144).

BRUSSELS

ALFA SABLON (££–£££)

Modern, efficient hotel with all amenities but no character in an area full of antique shops.
🔲 E8 ✉ 2–8 rue de la Paille
☎ 513 6040, fax 511 8141
🚋 Tram 91, 92, 93, 94

AMIGO (£££)

One of Brussels' finest hotels in the style of an 18th-century mansion perfectly located behind the Town Hall. Elegantly furnished rooms and extremely friendly staff. A favourite with ministers, opera singers and French media stars.
🔲 E7 ✉ 1–3 rue de l'Amigo
☎ 547 4747, fax 513 5277
🚇 Bourse/Beurs 🚌 34, 48, 94; tram 23, 52, 55, 56, 81

ART HOTEL SIRU (££)

A revamped 1930s hotel. Each room features work by a different Belgian artist. The higher you go, the better the views.
🔲 F6 ✉ 1 place Rogier
☎ 203 3580, fax 203 3303
🚇 Rogier

ASTORIA (£££)

This historic hotel near the Royal Palace was built in the 19th century for the reception of royal visitors. It's full of stories: the Aga Khan liked his bath filled with fresh milk, artist Salvator Dalí gave wild press conferences and French singer Serge Gainsbourg liked to hold court here. The palm trees, crystal chandeliers and mouldings are all still there, but modern facilities have been added.
🔲 F7 ✉ 103 rue Royale
☎ 227 0505, fax 217 1150
🚇 Gare Centrale/Centraal Station

AUBERGE ST-MICHEL (££)

Slightly scruffy hotel behind the grand gilded façade of the House of the Duke of Brabant. The furniture is worth putting up with in order to wake up with a view over one of Europe's most beautiful squares. Remember, though, that revellers on the Grand' Place can be rather noisy.
🔲 E7 ✉ 15 Grand' Place
☎ 511 0956, fax 511 4600
🚇 Gare Centrale/ Centraal Station 🚇 Bourse/Beurs
🚋 Tram 23, 52, 55, 56, 81

CONRAD (£££)

One of Brussels' finest modern hotels, on prestigious avenue Louise. The lobby, with huge chandeliers and marble floors, is a prelude to the luxurious rooms.
🔲 F9 ✉ 72 avenue Louise
☎ 542 4242, fax 542 4200
🚋 Tram 93, 94

FOUQUETS (£)

Basic but adequate rooms in the perfect location for Brussels' nightlife.
🔲 E7 ✉ 6 rue de la Bourse
☎ 512 0020, fax 511 9357
🚋 Tram 23, 52, 55, 56, 81

L'AGENDA (££)

Comfortable rooms and friendly service, close to avenue Louise. Reserve well ahead.
🔲 F9 ✉ 6 rue de Florence
☎ 539 0031, fax 539 00 63
🚇 Louise/Louiza 🚋 Tram 91

LA LÉGENDE (£)

Attractive courtyard hotel with a central location for Brussels' nightlife.

⊞ E7 ✉ 35 rue du Lombard
☎ 512 8290, fax 512 3493
🚌 Tram 23, 52, 55, 56, 81

LE DIXSEPTIÈME (£££)

Stylish hotel in the 17th-century former residence of the Spanish ambassador, with elegant rooms around a tranquil courtyard. Unlike any other Brussels hotel.

⊞ E7 ✉ 25 rue de la Madeleine ☎ 502 5744, fax 502 6424 🚇 Gare Centrale/Centraal Station

METROPOLE (£££)

Belgium's grandest hotel is a Brussels institution built in a mixture of styles in 1895. A favourite with film and media stars.

⊞ E6 ✉ 31 place De Brouckère ☎ 217 2300, fax 218 0220 🚇 De Brouckère
🚌 Tram 23, 52, 55, 56, 81

SLEEP WELL – ESPACE DU MARAIS (£)

This former YMCA offers comfortable rooms at hostel rates.

⊞ F6 ✉ 23 rue du Damier
☎ 218 5050, fax 218 1313
🚇 Rogier or Botanique
🚌 Tram 91, 92, 93, 94

BRUGES

BAUHAUS (£)

Popular central hostel with dormitories, triple, double and single rooms (free sheets and showers). Popular bar.

⊞ clll ✉ Langestraat 135
☎ 34 10 93, fax 33 41 80
🚌 6, 16

BED & BREAKFAST MARIE-PAULE GESQUIÈRE (£)

Comfortable rooms in an ivy-clad house overlooking a park by the city walls and windmills. Excellent breakfast with eggs and Belgian chocolate. The best place to stay in this price range.

⊞ cll ✉ Oostproostse 14
☎ 33 92 46 🚌 14

CATELINE (££)

This charming unusual hotel outside the centre is in a historic castle located in the Koude Keuken nature reserve.

⊞ Off map ✉ Zandstraat 272
☎ 31 70 26, fax 31 72 41
🚌 5, 15

DIE SWAENE (£££)

One of Bruges' most romantic hotels offers beautiful rooms furnished with plenty of lace – some with canal views. Very central but quiet and with attentive service and an exceptional restaurant that serves a delicious breakfast.

⊞ clll ✉ Steenhouwersdijk 1 (Groenerei) ☎ 34 27 98, fax 33 66 74 🚌 1, 6, 11, 16

DUC DE BOURGOGNE (££)

Slightly aged but comfortable rooms overlooking one of the most picturesque canals. Stylish traditional restaurant. Just ten rooms – if possible ask for one with a canal view.

⊞ blll ✉ Huidenvettersplein 12 ☎ 33 20 38, fax 34 40 37 🍴 Daily dinner; Wed–Sun lunch 🚌 1, 6, 11, 16

Hotel Grand Miroir

Brussels' oldest hotel was the Grand Miroir, dating from 1286 on the rue de la Montagne. Guests included Colette, Charles Baudelaire and Henri de Toulouse-Lautrec, who loved the brothels nearby. The hotel was eventually torn down in the 1950s; the Hotel Metropole carries on in the spirit of the Belle Epoque.

HOTELS

At home in Bruges

On holiday weekends, hotel rooms are scarce in Bruges. So many local residents offer bed and breakfast, often in quiet, residential areas but still within walking distance of the museums and sights. A brochure listing such accommodation is available from the tourist office. Reserve ahead.

✉ Burg 11, 8000 Brugge
☎ 44 86 86, fax 44 86 00

GRAND HOTEL DU SABLON (££)

Traditional, city-centre hotel with stained-glass art-nouveau dome. The rear part of the hotel was an inn 400 years ago but its pleasant rooms now offer all modern facilities.

✚ blll ✉ Noordzandstraat 21 ☎ 33 39 02, fax 33 39 08 🚍 All buses

HOLIDAY INN CROWNE PLAZA (£££)

This modern deluxe hotel on one of Bruges' prettiest squares was built over the foundations of the medieval Sint-Donaas Cathedral. Stylish, comfortable rooms, some with a lovely view of the square. Swimming pool.

✚ blll ✉ Burg 10 ☎ 34 58 34, fax 34 56 15 🚍 All buses

HOTEL AND PENSION IMPERIAL (£)

Pleasantly furnished rooms on a quiet street in the centre of Bruges and a lobby full of antiques and large bird cages.

✚ blll ✉ 24–28 Dweersstraat ☎ 33 90 14, fax 34 43 06 🚍 All buses

JACOBS (£)

A friendly family-run hotel in a quiet location less than ten minutes from the Markt.

✚ dlll ✉ Baliestraat 1 ☎ 33 98 31, fax 33 56 94 🚍 4, 8

MALLEBERG (£–££)

Well-maintained hotel in an old house just behind the Burg. TV available in every room.

✚ dlll ✉ Hoogstraat 7 ☎ 34 41 11, fax 34 67 69 🚍 All buses to the Markt

DE ORANGERIE (£££)

Elegant, tastefully decorated rooms in a renovated 15th-century convent covered in ivy and overlooking one of Bruges' prettiest corners. In summer, breakfast is served on the terrace by the canal.

✚ blll ✉ Kartuizerinnenstraat 10 ☎ 34 16 49, fax 33 30 16 🚍 1, 6, 11, 16

RELAIS OUD HUIS AMSTERDAM (££–£££)

Charming renovation of two 17th-century gentlemen's houses overlooking a quiet canal. The hotel is furnished with antiques and rooms are individually decorated.

✚ dlll ✉ Spiegelrei 3 ☎ 34 18 10, fax 33 88 91 🚍 4, 8

TER REIN (£–££)

Very well-placed 25-room hotel, five minutes from the centre. Friendly service and a good value, although the shower rooms are rather small. Some rooms have attractive canal views.

✚ dlll ✉ Langestraat 1 ☎ 34 91 00, fax 34 40 48 🚍 6, 16

DE TUILERIEEN (£££)

Spacious rooms in a renovated 16th-century mansion with views of the picturesque Dijver canal.

✚ blll ✉ Dijver 7 ☎ 34 36 91, fax 34 04 00 🚍 1, 6, 11, 16

BRUSSELS & BRUGES
travel facts

ARRIVING & DEPARTING

Before you go

- EU and Swiss citizens need a national identity card or passport for visits lasting up to three months. All other travellers need a visa. Visitors from USA, Japan Canada, Australia, New Zealand and some other countries need a valid passport but no visa.
- It is vital for all visitors to take out full health and travel insurance before travelling to Belgium.
- EU citizens are covered by reciprocal arrangments for medical expenses. Obtain an E111 form before travelling.

Climate and when to go

- Belgium's climate is temperate, with warm summers and mild winters. Snow is rare, though December and January can be cold and damp.
- When temperatures pick up, usually around Easter, more attractions open. In summer, café-terraces are open until late. Autumn is often rainy, but October can be beautiful.

Arriving by air

- The international airport is Zaventem, situated 14km north-east of Brussels. Flight information ☎ 753 3913 ⏰ 7ᴀᴍ–10ᴘᴍ
- The Airport City Express shuttle train runs between Zaventem and Brussels' main railway stations ⏰ 5:25ᴀᴍ–11:46ᴘᴍ every 20 minutes. The journey takes 30 minutes. For 24-hour information ☎ 723 2345. Regular trains leave for Bruges from Brussels' main station ☎ 555 2525. The journey takes one hour.
- Hourly buses to the Gare du Nord/Noordstation (35 minutes) leave from the first-floor level of the new terminal.

- Taxis outside the arrivals hall display a blue-and-yellow emblem, but they are expensive. Many accept credit cards but check with driver first.

Arriving by train

- Eurostar trains from London Waterloo arrive at the Gare du Midi in Brussels; journey time 3 hours 15 minutes, with 5 to 7 departures daily each way. Frequent trains to Bruges leave from the same station.
- The TGV train (Train à Grande Vitesse) from Paris also arrives at the Gare du Midi. There are five services daily.
- Direct trains connect all major European cities to Brussels, and there are also trains from Germany and Holland to Bruges.

Arriving by sea

- Belgium has extensive car ferry and jetfoil connections, with ports at Zebrugge and Oostende. There are fast and direct highway and regular rail rinks to both Brussels and Bruges. The Sally Line sea catamaran from Ramsgate to Oostende takes 90 minutes.
- Ferries from Dover (UK) to Calais (France) take 75 minutes, the hovercraft 35 minutes, with frequent services. Hoverspeed offers a bus connection from Calais to Bruges and Brussels.

Arriving by bus

- Eurolines buses connect all major European cities with Brussels. The international bus station is at CCN Gare du Nord/Noordstation ✉ 80 rue du Progrès ☎ 203 0707. There are frequent train connections from Gare du Nord to Bruges (one hour), which is the most efficient way for travellers to get to Bruges.

Customs regulations

- Provided it is for personal use EU nationals can bring back as much as they like, although the following guidelines should be adhered to as customs may wish to know why you are taking home more: 800 cigarettes, 400 cigarillos, 200 cigars, 1kg of tobacco, 10 litres of spirits, 20 litres of fortified wine, 90 litres of wine and 110 litres of beer.

ESSENTIAL FACTS

Electricity

- 220v AC. Plugs have two round pins. Some hotels provide adaptors for appliances from other countries.

Etiquette

- When you go out with Belgians to a café, it is customary to take turns buying rounds of drinks.
- Smoking in public places is banned, but allowed in restaurants, which rarely have no-smoking sections.
- If you are invited to someone's home, it is customary to take a gift of flowers or chocolates.

Money matters

- Belgian currency is the Belgian franc/frank, FB/BF.
- Coins: 1, 5, 20 and 50 francs.
- Notes: 100, 200, 500, 1,000, 2,000 and 10,000 francs.
- On 1 January 1999, the euro became the official currency of Belgium and the Belgian franc became a denomination of the euro. Belgian franc notes and coins continue to be legal tender during a transitional period. Euro bank notes and coins are likely to start to be introduced by 1 January 2002.
- Larger shops, hotels and restaurants accept credit cards.

- Banks exchange money. Out of banking hours, offices operate at main railway stations, in the Gare du Midi 🕐 7AM–11PM and Gare Centrale 🕐 8AM–9PM. Most banks will give cash advances on Eurocard/Mastercard or Visa. Several have offices at the airport.
- The American Express Gold Card Travel Service ✉ 2 place Louise ☎ 676 2733 and the American Express Travel & Financial Services ✉ 100 boulevard du Souverain ☎ 676 2626; 24-hour Customer Service 676 2121 issue traveller's cheques and deal directly with all stolen cheques or cards.

Opening hours

- Shops are usually open from 9 to 6 or 7 (there is no official closing time). Many shops in Bruges, fewer in Brussels, close for lunch (usually 12:30–2). Supermarkets and some grocery shops stay open until 9PM. The main shopping streets and areas stay open until 9PM one night a week, usually Friday.
- Banks open at 9AM and close between 3:30 and 5; some close for lunch.
- Post offices are open from 9 to 5, although the main office stays open later.
- Museums: Most are open from 9–4. Museums generally close on Monday in Brussels, on Tuesday in Bruges. Some also close for lunch, and some are open longer hours in the summer. Most museums also close over the Christmas holiday and some close on other public holidays. Phone first.

Places of Worship

Brussels

- Bruxelles–Acceuil: This service provides times of all the religious

89

services, in all foreign languages ✉ 6 rue de Tabora ☎ 511 8178

- Roman Catholic: St Anne's Church ✉ 10 place de la St-Alliance ☎ 345 5343 🕐 Masses in English Sat 5PM; Sun 10AM and 1PM 🚋 43

  St Nicholas ✉ rue au Beurre ☎ 513 8022 🕐 Mass in English Sun 10AM 🚋 Tram 23, 52, 55, 56, 81

- Anglican: Holy Trinity Church ✉ 29 rue Capitaine ☎ 511 7183 🕐 Services Sun 8:30AM, 10:30AM, and 7PM Ⓜ Louise/Louiza

- Jewish: Beth Hillel Liberal Synagogue of Brussels ✉ 96 avenue de Kersbeek ☎ 332 2528 🕐 English services Fri 8PM; Sat 10:30AM 🚋 54; tram 18, 52

Bruges

- St Peter's Chapel ✉ 't Keerske, Keersstraat 1 🕐 English service Sun 6PM 🚌 1, 2, 3, 4, 5, 6, 7, 8, 9, 11, 13, 15, 16, 17, 25.

Public Holidays

- 1 Jan: New Year's Day
  Easter Monday
  1 May: Labour Day
  Ascension Day (sixth Thursday after Easter)
  Whit Monday (seventh Monday after Easter)
  21 Jul: Belgian National Day
  15 Aug: Assumption
  1 Nov: All Saints' Day
  11 Nov: Armistice Day
  25 Dec: Christmas Day.
- If any of these days fall on a Sunday, the following Monday is a holiday.
- The Flemish community throughout Belgium also has a holiday on 11 July (Battle of the Golden Spurs), while Walloons (French speaking) have a holiday on 27 September to mark the end of the struggle for independence.

Student travellers

- Variable reductions are available on ticket prices in all state-run museums for holders of recognised international student cards.

Time differences

- Belgium is one hour ahead of GMT. (Central European Time plus 1 hour) lasts from the end of March until early October.

Toilets

- Public toilets are sometimes dirty. Tip attendants in bigger restaurants and cafés; the amount is posted on the wall.

Tourist offices

- Tourist and Information Office of Brussels (TIB) for maps, brochures, and hotel reservation service ✉ Town Hall, Grand' Place, ☎ 513 8940, fax 514 4538 🕐 Jun–Sep: Mon–Fri 9–7; Sat, Sun 9–1, 2–7. Oct–May: Mon–Fri 9–6; Sat, Sun 9–1, 2–6.
  Website: http//www.belgium-tourism.net.

- Toerisme Vlaanderen and OPT (Office for Promotion of Tourism for French-speaking Belgium) provides information on Bruges, Flanders and French Belgium ✉ 61 rue du Marché aux Herbe ☎ 504 0200 or 504 0300, fax 504 0270 🕐 Jun–Sep: Mon–Fri 9–;7 Sat, Sun 9–1, 2–7. Oct–Mar: Mon–Fri 9–6; Sat, Sun 9–1, 2–6.

- Toerisme Brugge ✉ Burg 11, Bruges ☎ 44 86 86, fax 44 86 00 🕐 Oct–Mar: Mon–Fri 9:30–5; Sat, Sun and hols 9:30–1:15, 2–5:30. Apr–Sep: Mon–Fri 9:30–6:30; Sat, Sun 10–12, 2–6:30. Website: http://www.brugge.be; e-mail: toerisme@brugge.be

Visitors with disabilities

- Public transport has few facilities but a minibus service equipped for wheelchairs is available at low cost from the public transport network STIB/MIVB (Société Nationale de Chemin de Fer de Belges/ Nationale Maatschapij Belgische Spoorwegen) ☎ 515 2365. On the trains outside Brussels, a passenger accompanying a disabled passenger always travels free.

PUBLIC TRANSPORT

Bicycles

- Cycling in central Brussels can be a pleasant way to explore the capital's environs. Be careful of traffic.
- Travelling around Bruges by bicycle is great. Outside the city, Damme is only 6.5km away, and Knokke or Zeebrugge less than 20km. Major railway stations sell combination tickets for train journey and bicycle hire. Or try:

Brussels:

Pro Velo ✉ rue de Londres 13-15 ☎ 502 7355

Bruges:

Station Brugge/Bagage ☎ 30 23 29

't Koffieboontje ✉ Hallestraat 4 ☎ 33 80 27

De Ketting ✉ Gentpoortstraat 23 ☎ 34 41 96

Bauhaus Bike Rental ✉ Langestraat 135 ☎ 34 10 93.

Maps

- As Brussels is bilingual, street names are marked in French and Flemish, with some metro stations in both French and Flemish. Only Flemish is used in Bruges. Pick up free transport maps, and timetables from tourist offices, the metro, STIB/MIVB (Société des Transports Intercommunaux de Bruxelles/Maatschapij voor het Intercommunaal Voerte Brussel) office in the Gare du Midi station, and the bus office at Bruges railway station.

Metro, buses and trams

- Brussels has an efficient public transport network with trams, buses and a metro system.
- Brussels metro stations are indicated by a white letter 'M'. Line 1A: Heysel to Hermann Debroux.

1B: Bizet to Stockel.

Line 2: Circle line from Simonis to Clémenceau.

Pré-Métro: from Gare du Nord to Gare du Midi and Albert.

STIB/MIVB ✉ 6th floor, 20 galerie de la Toison d'Or ☎ general information 515 2000 bus information 515 3064

- Bruges' efficient bus network makes it easy to leave the city centre. However, although this guide gives bus numbers for every sight, the centre of the city is small and it is easy to walk everywhere. Toll-free information line ☎ 059 56 53 53.

Taxis

- In Brussels, use only official taxis, marked with a taxi light on the roof. Taxis are metered and can be called or flagged down. Drivers are not allowed to stop if you are less than 100m away from a taxi stand. The meter price is per kilometer and is doubled if you travel outside the city ☎ 268 0000 or 349 4343
- In Bruges, taxi stands are on Markt ☎ 33 44 44 and at the railway station ☎ 38 46 60.

Trains

- Brussels has three main railway stations: Gare du Midi/Zuidstation, Gare Centrale/Centraal Station, and Gare du Nord/Noordstation. Two other stations, Schumann and Quartier Léopold, serve the European Union institutions, and the headquarters of NATO. Bruges has only one station near the city centre. Most Belgian cities are less than an hour from the capital (Brussels–Bruges about 55 minutes). Trains are reasonable, efficient and clean.
- Tickets are sold in stations, not on the train. Special offers are available on weekends and for day trips.
- Frequent trains from Brussels

91

centre run to the outlying areas and from Bruges to the coast.

- Train information: SNCB/NMBS Brussels ☎ 02-203 2880/203 3640 or for Bruges ☎ 38 23 82.

Types of tickets

- In Brussels the most economical way to travel is to buy ten tickets (*une carte de dix trajets*), five tickets or a 12-hour unlimited travel pass. A ticket is valid for one hour on bus, tram or metro and must be electronically stamped on the bus/tram or in metro stations. A one-day Tourist Passport, available from the tourist office on Grand' Place, also includes reductions on admissions to museums.
- In Bruges, an unlimited travel one-day pass (*dagticket*) is available for local buses.

MEDIA & COMMUNICATIONS

Mail

- Stamps are available from post offices and vending machines. There is a fixed rate for letters under 20g to any EU country; for non-EU countries charges depend on the weight and size of the envelope.
- Central Post Office ✉ 48a avenue Fosny, next to the Gare du Midi in Brussels ☎ 226 2310 ⏲ 24 hours
- Bruges post office ✉ Markt 5 ☎ 33 14 11 ⏲ Mon–Fri 9:30–5; Sat 9:30–1.

Newspapers and magazines

- Most European papers are sold on publication day at city-centre newsagents and at railway stations in Brussels and Bruges.
- The English-language *Bulletin* (published on Thursdays) has listings.
- Local papers such as the Flemish *De Morgen* and *De Standaard*, and

the French *Le Soir*, are available in both Brussels and Bruges and have more complete listings.

Telephones

- Some public phone booths are coin-operated, but many accept only prepaid telephone cards (20 or 105 units), available from post offices, stations, newsstands and supermarkets.
- International calls are expensive. Rates are slightly lower 8PM–8AM on Sundays and holidays.
- The international code for Belgium from the UK is 0032.
- The code for Brussels is 02, with the 0 omitted when dialling internationally, followed by a seven-figure number.
- The code for Bruges is 050, with the 0 omitted when dialling internationally, followed by a six-figure number.
- Use the initial 0 within Belgium but not when calling from another country.
- Faxes can be sent from any TT (Telephone/Telegraphe) office.

Television and radio

- TV programmes from France, UK, Germany, Holland and Italy can be received on cable. CNN and MTV are usually available.
- BBC World Service is on 648khz, Radio 4 on 198khz and Radio 5 live on 693/909khz. American Forces Network (24 hours) 101.7FM.

EMERGENCIES

Emergency phone numbers

- Ambulance/fire ☎ 100
- Police ☎ 101
- Brussels doctors on emergency call ☎ 479 1818/648 8000
- Bruges doctors on emergency call ⏲ Fri –Mon 8am–8pm ☎ 81 38 99.

Embassies and consulates
Brussels
- Australia ✉ Guimard Center, 6–8 rue Guimard
  ☎ 231 0500
- Canada ✉ 2 ave de Tervuren ☎ 741 0611
- Ireland ✉ 189 rue Froissart ☎ 230 5337
- New Zealand ✉ 47–48 boulevard du
  Régent ☎ 512 1040
- United Kingdom ✉ 85 rue d'Arlon
  ☎ 287 6211/287 6267
- USA ✉ 25–7 boulevard du Régent ☎ 508
  2111.

Lost property
- Report lost property immediately
  to the nearest police office or
  police headquarters. For insur-
  ance purposes always ask for a
  certificate of loss.
  Brussels ✉ rue du Marché au Charbon
  ☎ 517 9611
  Main railway lost propery ✉ Gare du
  Nord/Noordstation ☎ 55 2525
  Lost property on the metro ✉ inside
  Porte de Namur metro station next to Press Shop
  ☎ 515 2394
  Bruges ✉ Hauwerstraat 7 ☎ 44 88 44.

Medical treatment
- Standards of medical and hospital
  care are high. Most doctors speak
  French and English. Doctors see
  patients at their offices, but some
  will visit if you are too sick to
  move. Visits must be paid for in
  cash or by cheque. If the need
  arises the following hospitals provide 24-hour emergency
  assistance.

Brussels
- Hôpital Universitaire St-Luc
  ✉ 10 avenue d'Hippocrate
  ☎ 764 1111
- Hôpital St-Pierre ✉ 322 rue Haute
  ☎ 535 3111
- Hôpital Universitaire des Enfants
  Reine Fabiola (paediatric
  emergency room) ✉ 15 avenue Jean
  Cocq ☎ 477 3100.

Bruges
- Algemeen Ziekenhuis Sint-Jan
  Te Brugge ✉ Ruddershave 10 ☎ 45 21 11
- Algemeen Ziekenhuis Sint-Lucas
  ✉ Campus St-Lucas, St-Lucaslaan 29 ☎ 36 91 11.

Medicines
- Pharmacies (*Pharmacie/Apotheek*)
  are marked with a green cross and
  are open Mon–Fri 9–6. Each phar-
  macy displays a list of the
  pharmacies that are open outside
  these hours.

Sensible precautions
- Belgian law requires visitors to
  have 500Bf on them at all times,
  as well as an identity card or
  passport.
- Watch out for pickpockets and
  bag-snatchers in the crowded
  areas of Brussels and around railway stations.
- Avoid public transport at night in
  Brussels by taking a taxi.
- Belgium in general is as safe as
  other parts of Europe for women
  and lone travellers. Be careful in
  downtown Brussels, especially the
  red-light area around the Gare du
  Nord station, which can be
  dangerous at night.

LANGUAGE

- Belgium has a long history of
  language division and it is often
  better to speak English, which is
  widely understood. If you speak
  French to a Flemish person, he or
  she might be offended. If you
  happen to speak Flemish or
  Dutch to a French-speaking
  Bruxellois he will most certainly
  answer you in French with some
  disdain. It is hard to get it right,
  and even Flemish- and French-
  speaking people in Brussels will
  sometimes use English to
  communicate with each other.

INDEX

CityPack
Brussels & Bruges

Written by Anthony Sattin & Sylvie Franquet

Edited, designed and produced by
 AA Publishing

Maps © The Automobile Association 1997

Fold-out map © RV Reise- und Verkehrsverlag Munich · Stuttgart
 © Cartography: GeoData

Distributed in the United Kingdom by AA Publishing, Norfolk House, Priestley Road, Basingstoke, Hampshire, RG24 9NY.

The contents of this publication are believed correct at the time of printing. Nevertheless, the publishers cannot be held responsible for any errors or omissions or for changes in the details given in this guide or for the consequences of any reliance on the information provided by the same. Assessments of attractions, hotels, restaurants and so forth are based upon the author's own personal experience and, therefore, descriptions given in this guide necessarily contain an element of subjective opinion which may not reflect the publishers' opinion or dictate a reader's own experiences on another occasion.
We have tried to ensure accuracy in this guide, but things do change and we would be grateful if readers would advise us of any inaccuracies they may encounter.

A CIP catalogue record for this book is available from the British Library.

ISBN 0 7495 2349 2

Published by AA Publishing (a trading name of Automobile Association Developments Limited, whose registered office is Norfolk House, Priestley Road, Basingstoke, Hampshire RG24 9NY. Registered number 1878835).

Colour separation by Daylight Colour Art Pte Ltd, Singapore
Printed and bound by Dai Nippon Printing Co (Hong Kong) Ltd.

Acknowledgements
The authors would like to thank Nica and Willy Brouke-Diercx, Mr Drubble of the Bruges Tourist Office, Moeke and Leo Franquet, Pauline Owen and the Belgian Tourist Office, London, Jim Rowe and Eurostar, Irene Rossi, M. Serge Schultz of Hotel Metropole, Frank Vanderlinden and the many organisations who made our research a pleasure.
The Automobile Association would like to thank the following photographers, libraries and associations for their assistance in the preparation of this book: Mary Evans Picture Library 12, Memling Museum 42b; Musée d'Art Moderne 33; Spectrum Colour Library 5a, 7, 25a, 59, 87b; Groeningemuseum 45a, 45b. All remaining transparencies are held in the Association's own library (AA Photo Library) and were taken by Alex Kouprianoff.

Cover photographs
Main picture: Tony Stone Images; inset (a) Images Colour Library; inset (b) Zefa Pictures Ltd.

MANAGING EDITOR *Hilary Weston*